CASA MEXICANA STYLE

Photographs by
TIM STREET-PORTER

Text by
ANNIE KELLY

STEWART, TABORI & CHANG   NEW YORK

■ PAGE 1: A view over Lake Avandaro in Valle de Bravo from the Mascarenas house, designed by Manolo Mestre. PAGE 2: One of the original ruins of the Hacienda Puerta Campeche has been converted into a shallow swimming pool that flows through several rooms. PAGES 6–7: Duccio Ermenegildo's pool house for Alix and Goffredo Marcaccini features sleek built-in seating and pillows of hand-woven Mexican textiles.

Project Manager: Kate Norment

Designer: Anna Christian

Editor: Mary Christian

Production Manager: Jane Searle

Library of Congress Cataloging-in-Publication Data:

Street-Porter, Tim.
  Casa Mexicana style / photographs by Tim Street-Porter ; text by Annie Kelly ; foreword by Manolo Mestre.
    p. cm.
  ISBN-13: 978-1-58479-528-5
  ISBN-10: 1-58479-528-X
  1. Architecture, Domestic—Mexico. 2. Interior decoration—Mexico. I. Kelly, Annie, 1953- II. Title.

  NA7244.S78 2006
  720'.972—dc22

                                              2006007044

Published in 2006 by Stewart, Tabori & Chang
An imprint of Harry N. Abrams, Inc.

The text of this book was composed in Dante.

Printed and bound in China
10 9 8 7 6 5 4 3 2 1

HNA ■■■■■
harry n. abrams, inc.
a subsidiary of La Martinière Groupe

115 West 18th Street, New York, NY 10011

www.hnabooks.com

contents

foreword

MEXICO, A STATE OF MIND

■ Mestre and Street-Porter stumbled upon this rural *troje*, or primitive house, in Michoacán, discovered on their travels across Mexico. OPPOSITE: The active Volcán de Fuego, seen from the estate of the Hacienda de San Antonio in Colima.

MEXICO IS NOT ONLY A COUNTRY, IT IS A STATE of mind, as it refers to a culture with many rich memories. Before the arrival of the Spaniards Mexico had cities with a unique sense of urban design, found in the hundreds of archaeological sites like Chichén Itzá in the Yucatán Peninsula, Monte Albán in the valley of Oaxaca, and Teotihuacán in central Mexico. Sacred architecture for the soul and buildings for the gods embraced the surrounding landscape; it was architecture built to be lived in the open, where pyramids cast their long shadows at dawn and sunset.

Early in the sixteenth century—soon after the expulsion of the Moors in 1492 from the south of Spain and in the same year as the discovery of America—the Spanish conquered what is today known as Mexico. Moorish architecture had been rapidly incorporated into the Spanish sensibility, and with that freshness it arrived in New Spain, blending with the vernacular architecture and creating its own vocabulary.

The mixture of these two sensibilities creates the uniqueness of the casa Mexicana, a house that responds to the climate and blends with its surroundings. The illumination of the Spanish Renaissance also influenced and acquired weight in the expression of the buildings of this strange new country dotted with volcanoes.

Walls emerged as empty canvases onto which shadows are cast, creating the illusion of intricate carvings. This new architecture emerged from the earth and was built with the natural elements found in the area: adobe, stone, and sometimes a mixture that included porous volcanic stone to lighten the weight of the construction.

All the buildings in Mexico are shaped by generations of artisans who have found joy in their making, even up to the present day. Probably because death is always so present—sometimes we laugh at it—we cherish life, and this joy is always manifest in every single detail of our lives.

Mexican life is about emotions, about enjoying the rich quality of life, tequila in hand, watching a blood-red sunset by the sea, or feasting at an epicurean luncheon under the shade of a wooden pergola. It is about sensations: caressing a polished wall mixed with cactus juices, the sensation of silk, or of walking barefoot on a hand-chiseled cement-and-marble-dust floor.

We move from the inner to the outer space without noticing; a roof feels like a hat to protect us from the harsh sun in the tropics, allowing the air to flow through. Life is simple but sophisticated.

Mexican architecture is bold. It is grounded and sits comfortably on the earth, sometimes giving the sensation that it was even

En una ocasión me pidieron que disenara una casa que fuera mariposa y volara. . .
que fuera grillo y cantara. . . . Esta es la poesía que envuelve a la casa Mexicana.

carved from it. Visiting a Mexican market makes you also understand why color is so inherent to architecture and design.

The process of creation has a formal beginning geared toward spontaneity. At this moment the soul feels liberated and becomes purely emotional. Mystery, as architect Luis Barragán once said, invites us to discover what's behind the wall.

I remember driving in the Mexican countryside, during one of my many trips with Tim, and spotting a wooden shack dotted with flowers planted in motor-oil cans nailed to the wall. We knocked at the door and when it opened, a whole world of sensations appeared in front of our eyes—we were spellbound by the richness of information trapped in a simple 18-by-24-foot room.

As an architect I have explored the healing qualities in Mexican design that speak the language of joy, where color is always present. Once I was asked to design a house with the request that it be like a butterfly that could fly . . . like a grasshopper that could sing . . . . This is the poetry of the Mexican sensibility, a true casa Mexicana.

introduction

EL ARTE DE VIVIR

MEXICO IS A PASSIONATE COUNTRY. WHATEVER a Mexican's ancestral origins, whether Spanish, European, or even African (especially along the Caribbean coast), he is essentially Mexican first, and proud of it.

Unlike the United States, whose population is made up of a network of immigrant groups, the Mexican Mestizo culture, which derived from the original indigenous population, is the main influence across the country, a benchmark for the Mexicanism with which the whole of Mexico defines itself. It is this unifying force that has built such a strong culture and it pervades the rich Mexican sense of design and way of life.

The lifestyles of the great Mayan, Aztec, and Olmec cultures that dominated Mexico in the late fifteenth century, before the Spanish arrived, remain relatively the same. They lived chiefly on corn, beans, chilies, and tortillas, drank chocolate, and made *pulque* from the agave plant. The stone *metates* for grinding corn that have been unearthed by archaeologists are almost identical to those used in today's kitchens. The early Mexicans were largely vegetarian, but they also ate fish, turkey, and quail sparingly; like today, they enjoyed highly spiced food and finished their meals with a smoke of tobacco. In their marketplaces they sold honey, fruits and vegetables, vanilla, rubber, cotton, and pottery. They loved flowers and held many festivals and feasts, especially on religious holy days.

■ The gilded interior of an ornate church in Puebla. OPPOSITE: A Valle de Bravo flower seller prepares calla lilies for market.

Their houses reflected the climate and available materials, and were very similar to the simple village houses still common in rural Mexico. With no windows, they presented a blank facade of wood or stone to the street, topped by a thatched roof. Their doors were always open, although they were sometimes screened with a length of cloth hung with small bells. Aztec nobles lived in houses of red or whitewashed stone built around central courtyards that were filled with flowers and fountains. Windows were shaded with fabrics. Mexicans bathed often, and many houses had their own saunas or bathhouses.

When the Spanish arrived, they were amazed at the sight of the great city of Tenochtitlán (today's Mexico City), which was grander in scale than Madrid. The size, complexity, and sophistication of the architecture the Spanish found throughout Mexico—and which we still get a sense of when we visit the innumerable archaeological sites that dot the nation's landscape—laid a foundation for the country's enduring love of architectural expression that is so evident today.

In fact, the greatest creation of New Spain was its architecture. The Spanish were great builders, and in Mexico the union of Spanish traditional architecture with the skill of Indian craftsmen created a new style. At first the churches, for example, were Spanish, and the decorations were Mayan or Aztec, but over time they grew more graceful and the two traditions began to merge into a new local style.

Wheat, horses, cattle, pigs, and sheep were introduced by the Spanish, along with grapes and olives; however, the Mexican diet remained essentially the same. Five hundred years later, we can safely say that nowhere in the country are Mexicans in danger of losing their passion for food, music, color, and flowers. In city streets today musicians continue to play marimbas and sing *corridos*, and the colorful parades on religious feast days now transport likenesses of Christian saints instead of Aztec gods.

In many small towns houses still retain blank street facades that open onto plant-filled interior patios, while nearby markets brim with the same foods as in pre-Columbian days, beautifully laid out in colored rows.

In *Casa Mexicana Style* we have concentrated on four regions or types of architecture that show off the character and charm of

Mexican houses. A Mexican version of modernism can be found in the mountains around Mexico City and the Valle de Bravo. The next chapter is devoted to houses of San Miguel de Allende, which are typical of town houses throughout Mexico. Mexico's haciendas, the estates of landowners built from the seventeenth through the nineteenth centuries, are a mélange of styles based on Spanish and European estates, and their richness deserves a chapter. Finally, dwellings along the length of Mexico's Pacific coast share features that are instantly recognizable; they are the subject of the last chapter in this book.

Each of these styles, and the regional ways of life they accommodate, is a reflection of Mexican pride, and we who live outside Mexico have much to learn from the way this ancient culture has produced blueprints for living that are in such harmony with the human spirit.

Annie Kelly

■ The style of rural thatched-roof houses such as this one, on the Yucatán coast, has not changed for hundreds of years. OPPOSITE: A Zapotec Indian inspects fruit at a market in Oaxaca.

When Hernán Cortés and his lieutenants reached the crest of a hill and saw for the first time the high valley of Mexico embraced by the snow-capped volcanoes of Popocatepetl and Iztaccíhuatl, they were amazed. They saw cities and villages built in the water of a great lake, with temples and houses rising from the water like a vision. Without horses or carts, the Aztecs used water to transport people and supplies,

MEXICO CITY AND THE VALLE DE BRAVO

and the settlements were crisscrossed by gleaming canals that reflected the sky.

Today the lake is filled and in its place is the vast city of Mexico; the surrounding towns that the Spanish saw are its sprawling suburbs. Ecologically it is a disaster: it is the unfortunate result of uncontrolled development on a grand scale. Traffic swirls wildly around the crowded city; the polluted air together with the high altitude make it difficult to breathe.

But Mexico City is still full of treasures, with innumerable important and esoteric museums, archaeological discoveries, world-class architecture, and a rich cultural atmosphere. Here we found an apartment by Manolo Mestre that typifies the sophisticated urban Mexican way of life and an early and formative house that the great Mexican architect Luis Barragán designed for himself in Tacubaya.

A contemplative cross in the Capuchinas Sacramentarias chapel, designed by Luis Barragán. A private pier stretches out from a house on the lake in Valle de Bravo.

BARRAGÁN HOUSE

WHEN INTERNATIONAL STYLE MODERNISM arrived in Mexico, it took on a distinctly Mexican flavor, which one can see in almost every new building in Mexico. This can be traced to the influence of architect Luis Barragán, who is credited with bringing Mexican architecture and design into the twentieth century. He was able to accomplish this without rejecting Mexico's rich design heritage, which extends back over a thousand years.

In 1943 Barragán began building his own house in the Tacubaya district of Mexico City. During his first years as an architect he amassed many architectural ideas that had evolved while he was designing homes for other people, and this was a chance to experiment for himself.

"I wanted to feel that I was living in Mexico and I rejected all the false and overly decorated imported 'French' styles then in vogue," explained the architect in an interview with Alejandro Ramirez in 1962. "It is a house that expresses my own tastes and my sense of nostalgia and the idea of comfort."

Barragán was very involved in what made a house successful as a living space, especially its connection to the garden, and he saw the importance of defining attractive exterior spaces that became extensions of the interior living areas.

■ Barragán's iconic staircase seems to be suspended in air. OPPOSITE: His use of pink has influenced a whole generation of designers.

He failed to see the point of the large plate glass windows that other modernists liked to use on the street facade. He believed these took away from the essential privacy of the house, forcing people out and away from their homes. In his own designs, he shielded these windows from the street by using courtyard or patio walls, often painted in bright Mexican colors.

He furthered this sense of privacy in his house by orienting it inward, toward a large poetic garden at the back of the property. Barragán was also known for his landscape design, especially in the volcanic region of Mexico City called Pedregal, and he was able to give his garden a particularly inspired and contemplative quality.

On a quiet dead-end street in Tacubaya, the Barragán house blends in with all the others, distinguished only by a large window on the front facade. Set high up so it gives the interior a view of the sky, it represents an important design element of Barragán's work, the ability to bring light into a house while maintaining privacy.

He believed in eliminating unnecessary visual clutter, and the urban environment was no exception. Barragán often designed outdoor courtyards, even on the roofs of houses, with high walls admitting only the view of the sky. The rich blue of the sky was then incorporated into the colorful palette of the house, mixed with hot pink or bright yellow walls.

Probably one of the most copied elements in this house is in the double-height main room, where the "floating" stairway is held in place by careful construction inside the facing wall.

This master of modern architecture died in November 1988, but the house has been turned into the Casa Barragán Museum and is open to the public.

▓ This peaceful dining area looks onto the back garden. Barragán was first known as a landscape designer; the garden was always an important part of his architecture.

THOUGH IT WAS CREATED BY AN ARCHITECT who travels and works all around the world, Manolo Mestre's apartment looks as though he has never left home. "That's because my heart is in Mexico," he explains. "I want to show the dialogue between the periods of Mexican history that are part of my culture and heritage."

Many of his pre-Columbian artifacts were found during the construction of his many houses and buildings all over Mexico, but he has carefully collected the rest throughout his life.

Like most Mexican architects, Mestre is influenced by the country's particular brand of modernism, an architectural style that reaches back to Mexico's past. Many pre-Columbian ruins have the simplicity of modernist buildings, and the native use of bright colors has influenced the entire culture.

MESTRE APARTMENT

This apartment, built in the 1940s, is nestled on a quiet street in Lomas de Chapultepec, a modern neighborhood by Mexican standards, dating from the 1920s. Its basic simplicity drew the architect to its light-filled rooms, and Mestre reworked the spaces to suit his very urban life; to accommodate his love of entertaining; and to showcase his ever-expanding museum-quality collection of art, colonial furniture, books, and artifacts.

Mestre created low walls and screens of different strong colors throughout the main areas of the apartment; these change the spaces both visually and spatially. "All colors come from the ancient Aztec houses in Teotihuacán, which represent the comfort of the underworld life," he says.

■ A watchdog carved by an Indian shaman guards the entrance to the apartment. OPPOSITE: The raw silk of the living room sofa upholstery is accented with a Kuba textile pillow. The dark gray flannel wall is the perfect backdrop to Mestre's early paintings of Mexico and Teotihuacán and Olmeca stone masks.

■ An angled doorway in the entry hall leads to the living room. The dining room had no view, so Mestre created a lattice screen to provide light but hide his dressing room window next door. Mestre gave more architectural interest to the narrow passageway to the bedroom by lowering the ceiling with wood beams.

■ Sculptural shelves inspired by artist Donald Judd hold Mestre's sweaters and shirts in the dressing room. The master bedroom walls are upholstered in flannel, which cuts the noise of the city; the bed cloth is a souvenir from a recent trip to Indonesia. The room looks out onto a small garden.

He introduced light, color, and natural materials to the dining room by incorporating a painted wooden screen into the frame of the single large window that had no view, thus avoiding blinds and curtains that would have plunged the room into perpetual gloom.

Mestre is not afraid to use deep colors. His living-room walls are upholstered in a dark gray flannel, anchoring the space and creating a calm, orderly background for his paintings, statues, masks, and furniture. "It helps highlight the art," says Mestre, "and it gives the apartment a soft, peaceful quality, especially at night."

The gleam of silver candlesticks and gilded frames give this room a sumptuous but comfortable atmosphere, and the piles of books and magazines on the primitive wooden coffee table sit seductively next to a pillow-filled sofa upholstered in raw silk.

The private areas of the apartment are reached by a long corridor, hidden by a yellow wall. Mestre created the sense of an umbilical cord from the public to the private space by lowering the passage ceiling with lumber-grade wood painted red.

The master bedroom is a more private space. It is part of a trio of rooms that includes a dressing room permanently full of suitcases. Clothing is easy to find here, with sweaters and shirts resting on Donald Judd–inspired shelving. An inviting white hammock is strung up across the room, a reminder of the tropical beach houses that are some of Mestre's best-known projects.

The play of light throughout the day is one of the unexpected features of this apartment. Mestre has carefully considered each window, so walking along the length of the house becomes a different experience and discovery, depending on the time of day.

Like the inward-turning architecture of Luis Barragán, this apartment does not depend on its outside views, which makes it a quiet retreat from the busy city humming away outside.

VALLE DE BRAVO

■ The town of Valle de Bravo is at the edge of Lake Avandaro. OPPOSITE: Manolo Mestre designed this semicircular swimming pool to overlook a small valley near the town.

THE MOUNTAIN AIR IS FRESH IN FASHIONABLE Valle de Bravo, and smells of pine trees. This is reason enough for wealthy Mexican weekenders to flee the smog of gritty Mexico City for this mountain retreat. An easy ninety-minute drive through beautiful mountain scenery, Valle de Bravo is a stylish weekend resort built around a manmade lake. Several generations of Mexican families have built houses here, either scattered in the wooded hills that surround the water, or inside the charming colonial town, which is its focal point.

Local codes restrict house design to typically Mexican elements—tile roofs, stucco walls, and natural materials—to protect the rural character of the area. Many of Mexico's best-known architects have built houses here, including Ricardo Legorreta, José de Yturbe, Manolo Mestre, and Enrique Norten, who in designing his own weekend house was persuaded by the mayor to restrain his usual rigorously modernist aesthetic.

VALLE DE BRAVO'S BROAD AND BEAUTIFUL LAKE, dammed in the 1940s to produce hydroelectric power for Mexico City, transformed the original mining town into a resort, which is now a picturesque community of cobblestone streets packed with small shops and restaurants.

Manolo Mestre had already built nearly thirty houses in Valle by the time Guillermo and Olga Mascarenas asked him to trans-

MASCARENAS RESIDENCE

form their marshy half-acre lakeside plot on the outskirts of town. Although there are incredible views, it was still a challenge to build a house that could make the most of them while maintaining a sense of privacy from the neighboring houses, which cascade down the hill behind the site.

Mestre designed the stucco and wood house to embrace a front terrace that overlooks the lake, with a central swimming pool and with the main living areas to one side. He added a row of clerestory windows above the low-slung living room to add overhead light to the space. A lesser architect would have simply used a skylight, but Mestre was sensitive to the view of the house from above (it is overlooked by many houses, including others of his own design).

The Mascarenas house is modern with an organic feel. In the living room plaster surfaces abut a machete-carved *tepetate* stone wall. Above this, huge hand-hewn beams give the space scale and drama. Handwoven Mexican textiles and pottery establish the local flavor of the room, and Mestre added warm pine floors that step down to the natural terracotta tiles of the terrace outside. This outdoor space is furnished like the living room it really is; the mild

■ In the corner of the living room, plaster walls meet a machete-carved *tepetate* stone wall. Mestre designed the coffee table and the sofas, which are upholstered with hand-woven Mexican fabric. PAGES 34–35: From the lake, we can clearly see how Mestre designed the house around the pool to make the most of Valle's fresh air and sunshine.

climate of Valle is perfect for living outside, and the Mascarenas family takes full advantage of this during their brief stays away from smoggy Mexico City. Comfortable and casual *equipal* furniture, made of pigskin and wood, is arranged to invite lake-gazing or breakfast by the pool.

In the dining room, adjacent to a small country kitchen, an eighteenth-century antique carved wooden chest from Olga's family is surrounded by Mexican folk pottery that is integrated into the modern room by the use of natural materials and the hand-washed wall color. Even the modern lighting is hidden away, discreetly recessed into the ceiling. A stone and slate border on the floor in a Mixtec key pattern separates it from the terrace.

The other wing of the house contains the family bedrooms, which all have a view of the lake, framed by trees and foliage. The master bedroom was designed with a small fireplace, always welcome in Valle de Bravo, where evenings are often chilly due to the high altitude of the town. Windows frame a beautiful view of the lake and Cerro Gordo, a small extinct volcano.

■ A set of *equipal* furniture is laid out for a peaceful breakfast overlooking the lake. The guest beds, watched over by Mexican angels and a crucifix, have Oaxacan spreads and pillow fabrics by Cuna Indians of Panama.

CASA COLORADA

IN THE CASA COLORADA, BUILT IN 1996 NEAR Valle de Bravo, architect Ricardo Legorreta has succeeded in creating sculpture as well as architecture with this elegant house, regarded as one of his finest residential projects. The most distinguished architect of his generation in Mexico, Legorreta has built houses, museums, and commercial buildings all over the world.

■ The circular forecourt of the house has a grand sculptural quality. OPPOSITE: The long entry passage is paved with antique granite slabs, and the textured walls relate to the exterior.

In partnership here with his architect son Victor, Legorreta was able to show his mastery of architectural form and his knowledge of Mexican materials, especially in the dramatic forecourt and entry. Built for a Mexico City family, the house is reached through an avenue of pine trees, ending dramatically at a cobbled motor court. This takes the form of an elegantly curved courtyard, paved with a circle of bricks punctuated by a central stone carved in a labyrinth design.

From here, steps lead down to the entrance of the house through carefully articulated stucco walls. A second entry courtyard is reached by broad stone steps that continue onto a causeway across shallow pools lined with river stones. Here the architect installed carved stone entrance doors, emphasizing the only building material used in this dramatic and sculptural approach to the house.

■ LEFT TO RIGHT: A small door in the wooden grille opens for more view. Masterful proportion governs this passage joining several bedrooms. The path out the front door is flanked by two shallow pebble-filled pools; it is kept private by the high garden walls at the top of the steps. An indoor pool with a glazed roof provides a shock of color inside the house.

These doors lead to an open corridor that runs the length of the central living room and continues through to a two-story bedroom wing. This living room is a dramatically serene space, with thick hand-hewn beams supporting the ceiling. Two fireplaces, one at each end, keep this room warm in Valle's chilly alpine evenings. A door opens from here onto the indoor swimming pool, which has been painted in blasts of color; there water acts as an illusory floor to the room. The architects designed the interiors and also the garden, creating a coordinated design vision inside and out.

Legorreta studied in Mexico City, and has been in business as an architect for over forty-five years. This house has the practiced hand of a master, who says modestly: "Mexico is a country of architects. Architecture is one of the pillars of our culture and part of our daily life: every Mexican is an architect at heart."

LAKESIDE HOUSE

DIEGO VILLASEÑOR IS KNOWN FOR HIS DRAMATIC coastal architecture that incorporates natural materials from the forests and the earth. Here he brought the spirit of the ocean to this lakeside country house at Valle de Bravo.

The site was unusual: a lizard-shaped peninsula that overlooks the water and is surrounded by mountains. Villaseñor was the natural choice for this weekend house, as his clients already lived in one of his early houses in Mexico City.

No Mexican architect can escape the influence of Luis Barragán, however subtle, and Villaseñor has absorbed those lessons well in his strong use of color to emphasize the forms of the architecture and the open feeling of space. These combine to make this house a wonderful experience for both the owners and their large family of five grown children.

Margarita Alvarez designed the interiors with sympathy for the architecture, bringing even more natural materials into the house by hanging clay pots on the walls, using dried cactus as a side table, covering sofas in jute, and introducing leather *equipal* furniture.

The house looks across at a lakeside view of Valle de Bravo. Villaseñor stepped the property down the gentle slope

A roof terrace overlooking the lake and town of Valle de Bravo has a low *equipal* bench filled with cushions. On the bench sits a jug of jamaica made from hibiscus flowers.

of the peninsula toward the lake and its view of the old town. The swimming pool floats above the lake, separated from it by a small stretch of greenery.

The house wraps around an ancient oak tree that is overlooked by each of the main rooms, while the master suite and second-floor study are off to one side of the house. All the main rooms also open onto terraces, while the outdoor dining terrace is roofed and overlooks the lake. Modern tropical landscaping surrounds the house, and everywhere in the house there is a sense of living with nature.

The open terrace of the house offers many shady corners or sunny spaces for relaxation by the pool. The dining room's high-pitched ceiling, supported by large wooden beams, lets in a sun-washed swath of color that highlights a striking collection of pots made by the Tarahumaran Indians of Chihuahua.

DE YTURBE HOUSE

BUILT INTO A HILLSIDE THAT DESCENDS
steeply toward the Valle de Bravo lakeshore, this house by architect José de Yturbe interacts with a series of strong outdoor spaces.
Broad steps descend from the initial parking area into a walled
courtyard that has the artful spareness of a stage set, animated by
a tree, a stone sphere balanced arrestingly on the bottom stair, and
two ceramic pots. Large perforated iron doors, whose hinges are
hidden in a deep recess, open into a loggia and a broad terrace, with
the lake as a picture-perfect backdrop. At one end of the loggia is a
sitting area, arranged next to a circular fireplace; such a cozy setting
is welcome when the fresh mountain air brings chills after dusk.

▓ Pots of orange
impatiens fill the
spacious pebble-lined
tile terrace with a view
of the dramatic cliffs of
La Peña. Broad perforated
iron doors swing open
to reveal a loggia and
broad terrace. Wide steps
descend from the parking
area into the walled
loggia.

At the other end of the terrace, a pigskin-covered *equipal* table and chairs, sheltered by a tree, have a view of the serene lake. A low balustrade—only twelve inches high—stretches the length of the terrace, tautly delineating the expanse of lake beyond. The terrace, with its deep-set loggia to give shade during the heat of the day, serves as a giant living room. For cold or rainy days there is a snug sitting room inside.

In front of the bedroom wing an infinity-edged swimming pool is set lengthwise into an adjoining patio so as not to disturb the tranquility of the main terrace. This is overlooked by bedrooms on two levels; the second is reached by a distinctive yellow-walled stair. The house is generously proportioned; the scale of its rooms and the simple purity of its detailing, influenced by seventeenth-century haciendas, creates an atmosphere of serenity and graciousness.

■ The earth-colored sofas surrounding the coffee table in the comfortable living room are surrounded by a collection of Mexican art on white stucco walls. A mosquito net over the bed and a white wing chair lend an intimate scale to the bedroom's dramatically high, beamed ceiling.

Famous for its picturesque charm and cobblestone streets, San Miguel de Allende looks like a village from the South of France to which someone has taken a colorful paintbrush with a brilliant palette of colors. One of the prettiest and most popular sixteenth-century colonial towns of Mexico, it is perched on an old pre-Columbian hill town, surrounded by dry, dusty mountains between Mexico City and the quiet manufacturing town of León in the central state of Guanajuato.

SAN MIGUEL DE ALLENDE

Charming hotels pack the historic center of this World Heritage site, which is rich with exquisite seventeenth- and eighteenth-century buildings. San Miguel is teeming with restaurants, antique shops, and sophisticated design stores that can be found right alongside colorful local vendors supplying saddles, bridles, and supplies for the busy Mexican rural life in the surrounding countryside.

San Miguel de Allende was founded in about 1542 to protect and safeguard travelers from attacks by the indigenous and aggressive Chichimeca Indians on the Antigua Camino Real, a silver route between Zacatecas and the capital, Mexico City, then center of the kingdom of New Spain.

Originally called San Miguel El Grande, after its founder, the Franciscan monk Juan de San Miguel, the town became San Miguel de Allende in 1826 in honor of General Ignacio Allende, an important hero of the Mexican War of Independence who joined the army in San Miguel and led it to several important victories over the Spanish.

There are many outstanding buildings in San Miguel. The house where Ignacio Allende was born is a good example of the city's baroque architecture; today it serves as the regional museum. La Casa del Mayorazgo de la Canal has a lovely neoclassical facade,

■ CLOCKWISE FROM ABOVE: Amid flowering jacaranda trees, the spires of the 18th-century church of La Parroquia dominate the view of San Miguel de Allende. A typically ornate window detail of one of the private houses in San Miguel. A restaurant in the town square. An ancient chapel door is decorated for Holy Week.

while the old ancestral home of Don Manuel Tomás de la Canal, dating from 1735, houses the Instituto Allende with its inner patios, a graceful chapel, and beautifully proportioned arches.

The chapel of Santa Cruz del Chorro, one of the oldest in town, dates from the beginning of the seventeenth century, while the lovely complex of the church and oratory of San Felipe Neri was built in the early eighteenth century. The pink stone baroque facade of this church sparkles in the strong daylight, and its interior is richly decorated with carved furniture, sculptures, and moving religious paintings.

Among the most striking buildings here is the eighteenth-century church of San Francisco, with its extravagantly ornamental churrigueresque facade. Visible from many vantage points around the town, it was built on the foundations of an even older seventeenth-century church, and has become a hallmark San Miguel de Allende view.

By 1900 San Miguel de Allende started a gradual decline. Stripped of mineral resources, its unique beauty was nonetheless

recognized, and it was declared a national monument in 1926. That farsighted effort has protected its fine colonial architecture, and by the 1950s it became a popular destination for its natural hot springs and the preserved beauty of the town. The Mexican entertainer Cantinflas made San Miguel fashionable in the 1950s and '60s, and the Instituto Allende, founded in 1950, was American-accredited, so it brought students from the United States as well as the rest of Mexico.

In the late eighteenth century San Miguel de Allende was one of the richest towns in all of the Americas, and many grand colonial houses have been restored to provide very comfortable housing in this charming little town. This, and the mild year-round climate, has attracted many expatriates who have helped protect San Miguel, making it one of the best small villages in North America.

The antique fireplace in Gerry McCormack and Leslie Tung's living room has a pair of white linen armchairs on either side. The Casa Midy tray holds a collection of local pottery used as candle-holders. OPPOSITE: Easter celebrations in San Miguel de Allende.

CASA MIDY

The guest bedroom is reflected in the bathroom mirror. A white Casa Midy lantern sits on the original tile floor and the nearby column opens to reveal shelves with bath linens. PAGES 58–59: The living room's large daybed, upholstered in fabric found at a French flea market, sits across from a pair of French-inspired Mexican armchairs. The pull-out coffee table and the metal Varenne chair are Casa Midy designs.

"IN OLD MEXICAN HACIENDAS, THE WHITE limestone walls were highlighted with just a few pieces of old furniture," explains Anne-Marie Midy, "and I wanted to keep the fresh feeling of these beautiful old buildings."

This is exactly the mood of the house she shares with her Mexican husband and partner, Jorge Almada, in the center of San Miguel de Allende. It has the usual large wooden entry door and deep-colored facade of a San Miguel town house, but once you are inside, the interiors are fashionably pale. At first sight, the house appears to be filled with French furniture; this is just an illusion, however, as almost everything in the house is completely Mexican. Midy is French, but after meeting Almada in New York, she moved with him to Mexico, and they now live happily together in San Miguel with their young son, Olivier.

A glimpse of the press clippings on their web site shows how successful their design company, Casa Midy, has been; their furniture, objects for the home, and decorating have been featured in many of the world's best interior design magazines. They moved to San Miguel de Allende to be able to work directly with the talented and diverse artisans of Mexico, and thanks to the internet have found a market for their work in that country and abroad.

As you enter the house directly from the busy street, a charming clutter of furniture in the entry hall—waiting to be shipped to expectant clients all over the world—is watched over protectively by an eighteenth-century colonial painting from San Miguel. The rest of the walls are hung with white plaster molds that Midy found in an old San Miguel factory, which she and her friend Leslie Tung sell at their nearby shop, Mitu. This small shop sells both antique and new household objects, selected pieces from the Casa Midy inventory, and unique designs developed specifically for Mitu.

Midy explains that the back of her front door was very plain, so she covered it with *ex-votos*, *milagros*, and *retablos*—"together costing much more than a new door," she laughs.

This room leads into a combined living and dining room, which overlooks their central courtyard. The living end of the room is gathered around a fireplace flanked by a pair of built-in book-

■ LEFT TO RIGHT: Jicky rests in front of the courtyard fountain. Zyka and Toka take over the master bed beneath a photograph by Jorge Almada, taken at a local iron workshop. The doorway in the front entrance gives a view past the living/dining room to the courtyard. The courtyard makes an inviting outdoor dining space.

cases, topped by plaster conchas. The furniture is all Mexican and includes one of Casa Midy's most popular wire chairs, the Varenne opera chair, upholstered in dark brown leather. The large organic watercolor giving height to the room is by San Miguel artist Mari-José Marine.

Almada and Midy entertain often in the casual way of modern, busy people. Overlooking the dining corner of this room is a large statue of a saint, surrounded by a nineteenth-century altarpiece, finds from San Miguel's many wonderful antique shops. The Casa Midy Hacienda table was inspired by old tin Mexican store counters, and it is big enough to seat most of their friends; it doubles as an impromptu workspace if needed.

The courtyard, landscaped with white gravel and gray-white olive trees, has a beautiful simplicity. Next to a fountain is a set of outdoor chairs and a dining table, creating an inviting, watery space for warm evenings.

On a landing near the courtyard sits a small Mexican cupboard filled with tools for the garden. Sun streams into the master bedroom sitting area, which surrounds a small fireplace. The metal Casa Midy coffee table contrasts with a 19th-century wood chair, a Mexico City discovery.

At the back of the courtyard is a large studio living room where Almada creates his Casa Midy furniture. The comfortable sofas are usually claimed by the couple's three dogs, who like the breezes from the open courtyard doors. The round silver coffee table is another Casa Midy prototype.

Up winding stairs are the family quarters, a big master bedroom that doubles as another living room, furnished with a French-style sofa that Midy upholstered in brown velvet and a nineteenth-century chair discovered in a Mexico City flea market. Above the bed is a large bird photograph by Almada, which adds color and life to the room. A stunning old large rustic bookcase still has its original paint. It was another local find, and it has a simple and dignified presence, filled with antique books and family photos and flanked by a set of hanging lamps that Midy designed.

Midy also works in this room, at an antique desk from where she can peer out through the trellis of the adjoining balcony to a beautiful view of San Miguel de Allende and the eighteenth-century church of La Parroquia. In the adjoining master bathroom Almada installed an old tile mural from the 1920s, showing the Almada family hacienda La Primavera, which produced sugar in the state of Sinaloa. His family has a venerable Mexican heritage: his great-grandfather, Plutarco Elias Calles, was the president of Mexico in the 1920s, and formed what is now known as the PRI in 1929.

The age of their house is hard to judge. Like many houses in San Miguel, it has been reworked over the centuries so all that is left of its eighteenth-century origins is the exterior. Almada believes much of the house was rebuilt in the 1960s, and they have added to the improvements, especially with the installation of big, sunny windows overlooking the central courtyard, which has brought much more light into the house.

BACK IN 1780, BISHOP SOLLANO OF THE PARISH of San Miguel de Allende built a handsome town house for himself with a commanding view overlooking the valley below. These were good times for San Miguel, and his house reflected the prosperity of this growing colonial city, with its high ceilings, beautiful stone walls, and eloquent proportions. Today, with recent sympathetic renovations by its new owner, Dorsey Gardner, a financial adviser from Boston, Sollano's eighteenth-century town house will continue well into this millennium.

Gardner hired Anne-Marie Midy of Casa Midy to carry out the renovations. He usually restores his own houses, but he had seen some of her work locally and loved her use of color and fabrics. He

GARDNER HOUSE

also hired Sebastian Zavala as the renovating architect. Instructions to his decorator were refreshingly simple. "He asked only that the house not be too predictably Mexican," says Midy. "Although everything in it is from Mexico, it is just a bit more sophisticated than usual."

From the street, the house opens into a large courtyard, where Midy added a fountain and water trough to cool the air. Banners of jute suspended overhead shade the courtyard from the harsh midday sun. The living rooms open onto this area and are screened by an arcade that runs along two sides. Here Zavala added well-proportioned stone columns from a local quarry. A second, lower courtyard leads to a small painting studio and a lower garden, where Midy added another water trough and outdoor seating.

■ A wooden church bench sits on the entry courtyard loggia. The back of the bench was replaced with wire mesh.

Banners of jute shade the courtyard from the midday sun. The lower courtyard can be glimpsed through the arch. OPPOSITE PAGE: The arch between the two courtyards and a view of the stairs leading to a guest room. The entry courtyard holds a fountain and long stone trough.

Midy brought her French sensibility to the project. The main building, where Midy kept a pale palette, has a peaceful and contemplative quality. "Many people," she believes, "who move to San Miguel forget the subtlety of color and go straight to primary colors. You have to be careful not to have your dream house looking like a tourist restaurant."

In fact, Midy's restraint is exactly what captures the delicate beauty of this house. She has thought carefully about the overall atmosphere of the rooms, and respected their age with subtle combinations of old and new furnishings. The new furniture was either made specifically for the house or taken from her Casa Midy line, which is also designed by her partner, Jorge Almada.

The beautiful original back stone wall of the study, at the front of the house, was left bare, and Midy stripped the antique cupboards behind the desk to give them more character. A green glass bottle was made into a lamp, and a copper shade was added; this combination of color, texture, and surface gives a rich luster to the entire room.

The main living room, next door, has street views discreetly shaded by blinds and beamed ceilings hung with overscaled linen light fixtures designed by Midy, a dramatic and economical way to add lighting. Low elegant furniture suits this room, and the orange-yellow colors of the linen upholstery and Casa Midy leather table keep the space to a natural, earth-toned palette. All the paints for the house are lime wash, custom mixed at the site.

■ PAGES 68, 69: Blue mercury glass vases, made into lamps, give lustrous color to this upstairs guest bedroom. The master bedroom still has a trace of an original frieze running along the top of the wall. The linen ceiling lamps used throughout the house were designed by Anne-Marie Midy.

Zigzag Talavera tiles give the kitchen graphic punch. Under a row of handmade Mexican tile, a welcoming green bench sits in the entryway to the house.

■ The main living room
fireplace was added to the
house. A long row of votive
candles light the dining
room table.

The master bedroom was created from three smaller rooms
that formed a wing of the house. Traces of an ancient frieze still
remain at the top of the thick, beautifully plastered bedroom walls.
Again, simplicity is an important feature of this room: the bed has
custom-made pale blue linens, and the sole chair is slipcovered in
off-white linen.

Midy found a tall nineteenth-century standing mirror that has
a sculptural presence in its position in the adjoining dressing room.
She added a big mirror to the bathroom, made out of square mirror
tile, and again used her linen lamps, repeated here as throughout
the house, to add drama and texture to the room.

The kitchen is reached by a set of outdoor steps at the back of
the main building. It is convenient to the two outdoor dining areas
below, as well as the dining room off the main courtyard. The warm
red ocher of the kitchen contrasts well with the brightly graphic
blue and cream Talavera tile, which zigzags its way past the stainless
steel restaurant-quality stove.

For the dining room Midy sheathed an antique rustic table
with stainless steel and added metal chairs with cream linen seat
pads from the Casa Midy range of furniture. Long rows of votive

■ A wire vase from Mitu is filled with olive leaves. The office has a view of the street; its wall was stripped to reveal ancient stone. A lamp made from a copper shade on a green glass bottle adds drama and scale.

candles in an old molasses mold on the table add evening drama. While carefully leaving one wall neutral so as not to overwhelm the room, she gave the rest of the space a rich blast of red ocher.

Midy also designed a stone dining table for the outdoor space in the lower courtyard below the dining room. She explains how accident had a hand in its final design: "It broke in two when the workmen carried it in, and we decided to keep it in two pieces. After all, it still works!"

For additional outdoor entertaining, Zavala created a loggia out of an existing separate building in the back garden. Here he added a fireplace of antique stone, which is surrounded by more Casa Midy seating, this grouping made of strips of woven leather.

Gardner likes to paint, and he has a studio that looks onto the garden and is well lit. A day bed and a large-scale bookcase, which Midy found locally, anchor the room.

With Zavala's help, Gardner added a top-floor guest suite over the kitchen to take advantage of the buildings' spectacular upper-level views over San Miguel. With a comfortable bedroom and a rooftop whirlpool tub, this is an ideal place to watch the sun set over the town.

■ The dressing room's 19th-century mirror was found in Mexico City. The pressed tin headboard in an upstairs guest room is from the Casa Midy Hacienda Collection. The *armario* in the entryway is made from local mesquite wood; the horse on top was found in San Miguel. The wall paint was mixed with local earth for authentic color.

IRISH ARCHITECT GERALD McCORMACK AND designer Leslie Tung claim they had no plans at all to move to San Miguel when they arrived for a week's visit about ten years ago. They were even thinking about moving to Europe from New York, and were only taking a short vacation from their busy and complicated lives in the United States. Instead they fell in love with San Miguel de Allende, and bought a small rundown property for what they told themselves was to be a vacation house.

The single-story building, which dates from the 1800s, was a little small, so McCormack decided to add a top floor and a matching building at the rear of the property, now reached by a colorful open courtyard, to maximize the living spaces.

McCORMACK AND TUNG HOUSE

For the courtyard McCormack designed a small fountain to keep the air fresh, and kept a large old pomegranate tree that was somehow still flourishing when they bought the house.

He based the new work on the proportions of the old, keeping the ceiling height of the original building. Matching the new with the old was less of a challenge than he expected: "Even the early colonial buildings were very simple, almost modern," McCormack explains.

Renovations became more extensive than they had imagined, and the couple found themselves spending more and more time in San Miguel. So it was only a matter of time before they fell completely under the spell of the town's notorious charm. Before they knew what they were doing, they were shipping their furniture from New York and settling into the pleasant rhythms of small-town life.

■ The main living room fireplace of the 19th-century house has a row of antique Asian statues on the mantle piece, which is flanked by plaster molds from the owner's collection. The armchair has been slipcovered with washed linen.

Leslie then opened Mitu on a nearby street with designer Anne-Marie Midy—whose home and designs are included in these pages. The shop, selling antiques and Mitu designs, also houses small art exhibits. McCormack opened an architectural practice in his new building at the rear of the house. It makes an ideal studio, as it is peacefully distant from the noisy street. And they don't seem to miss New York at all.

An antique Mexican side table holds a collection of plants in blue and white Mexican pots. Gerry McCormack designed this central courtyard fountain, which cools both sides of the house. The wall is painted blood orange to define the outdoor space from the surrounding house.

THE TOWN OF SAN MIGUEL IS A BIG COLORFUL patchwork of houses and inner gardens, and when Spook and Jamie Stream were lucky enough to find several properties together, they had the unusual opportunity to start with raw land that was as wide as the space between two town streets.

CASA STREAM

Jamie explains, "We were just visiting friends in San Miguel, and happened across this great piece of property so close to the center of town, that was once basically a couple of ordinary houses from the 1950s."

It struck her that a house here would be a perfect place to entertain friends and family as "it would be so easy just to walk into town," she laughs, "and give them all plenty to do."

This wasn't their first house in Latin America. Spook Stream's family originally came from Spain, and they had a large family house in Antigua, Guatemala, where they had both grown to love the beauty, climate, distinctive culture, and people of Latin America.

They realized that this would be a perfect place to foster their enthusiasm for Latin American art and house their constantly expanding collection of paintings. They also couldn't bear to part with their antique Spanish colonial furniture from Guatemala. Jamie explains how they envisioned a new home that would combine the best of both worlds, or two eras: "We wanted a fresh, modern house in San Miguel that also incorporated the old, like our art collection which mixes both old and new."

Their garden winds around several reconstructed buildings and swimming pools, giving the impression of an even larger property. Its peaceful tranquility makes it hard to believe that they are nearly next door to the colorful and busy center of town.

The house is entered by a series of small outdoor and indoor courtyards. The main living room is very dramatic, with a double-

■ The loggia was crafted from some of the original walls found on the property. This outdoor entertaining area overlooks one of the two swimming pools.

The fireplace is adorned with two hanging Mexican silver braziers; underneath is a chair upholstered in pale green silk with a panel of silk damask draped over the back and an 18th-century chair covered in Fortuny fabric.

height ceiling lit during the day from above with the soft light of skylights. Fabric cascades down the walls to frame tall French doors on three sides of the room and the fireplace is flanked by two hanging Mexican silver braziers. The decorators brought in the local firm of Casa Midy to help with the furniture, and they created the central table in white leather, which is loaded with books on Mexico.

Beyond this room, which overlooks one of the two swimming pools, is an outdoor enclosed terrace created from existing buildings. These ancient walls provide a beautiful backdrop to this area, which can be used as a living and dining space, with steps leading down to a second small swimming pool. Jorge Almada and Anne-Marie Midy of Casa Midy supplied chairs and tables here and throughout the garden; their furniture designs add a sophisticated touch to the landscaped grounds.

Spenser Sutton, the Streams' architect based in New York, carefully created outdoor spaces as a series of courtyards in the peaceful garden, which they use for meals and relaxation. "We somehow have at least ten for lunch every day," says Jamie Stream.

▨ This peaceful guest room overlooks the garden. The 17th-century-style beds are covered in brown and cream linens with orange pillows. The lamp, made from a Spanish colonial figure, sits on an 18th-century Italian cabinet.

Just a glimpse of a Mexican hacienda is enough to stir the imagination: surrounded by thousands of acres, they were usually beautifully and dramatically placed in the countryside. For some, like the Hacienda de San Antonio, the main view was a smoking volcano, for others, a beautiful landscape. They were all meant to convey power and authority and their builders recognized that a sense of drama would help make this possible.

THE HACIENDA

Surrounded by high walls and well-planned gardens with lawns and clipped hedges, a hacienda offers a seductive rural life in perfect isolation from the outside world, accompanied by cowboys, horses, and dogs, and punctuated by long lunches served on broad terraces with plenty of tequila and Mexican beer.

The hacienda system in Mexico began with rewards bestowed on the famous conquistador Hernán Cortés in 1529 from a grateful

■ The *hacendado* of San Juan Tlacatecpan in Teotihuacán. This hacienda has a hospitably large dining room with a traditional vaulted brick roof.

Spanish crown. For his success in overthrowing the powerful Aztec and Mayan kingdoms with just a handful of soldiers, he was given the title marquis of the Valley of Oaxaca as well as the initial land grant of much of what is now the state of Morelos. This established a pattern of land ownership for the ruling Spaniards that also included absolute rights over the inhabitants of the lands, which was an indirect governmental form of control. Large country properties were given to members of the Spanish military as a way of administering the new colony, not unlike the manor system set up by William the Conqueror after 1066 in England.

As the conquistadors and early colonizers began to mark out their territory, the Church, and especially the Jesuits, were also granted vast hacienda holdings, which provided them all with common interests, creating a powerful class of rulers.

These controls were reflected in the design of the haciendas. As the landed estates of Mexico, they were built to the highest design standards, and are a legacy of architectural beauty, strength, and refinement, with the added surprise and mystery of being inevitably located in the most unexpected rural surroundings.

They specialized in regional products, such as sugar, mescal, pulque, tequila, sisal, cotton, and cattle, and sometimes stretched for miles in every direction. Isolated as they were, they became like small towns, with schools, churches, shops, and even hospitals. Their owners rarely visited, preferring to live opulently in Mexico City and Paris, but when they did return it was to resume a similar lifestyle in the country, and the hacienda came alive again, with lavish parties, bullfights, and balls.

The hacienda system was abolished in Mexico in 1917, after the revolution, and the owners were stripped of much of their land. Some survived because the ties to the families who owned them were too strong to abandon, while others were still profitable despite their reduced size.

Today the remaining haciendas are valued for their architectural beauty and continue as private family estates or small hotels. Many are in ruins, giving a poetic touch to their former grandeur, and providing glimpses of a colorful past.

THE STATELY HACIENDA DE SAN ANTONIO IS a place of fantasy and magic that seems as remote and exotic as Bolivia or Argentina, despite a flight of only two hours from the United States, and a scenic cross-country drive from either Guadalajara or Manzanillo.

HACIENDA DE SAN ANTONIO

A caballero waits at the entrance of the Hacienda de San Antonio. Behind him runs the volcanic stone aqueduct that supplies water to the hacienda gardens. PAGES 90–91: The main hacienda building has a grandstand view of the Volcán de Fuego.

The first view of the main house, overlooking a broad, rushing river, shows it dramatically surrounded by a ring of mountains. In the background, but dominating everything, the majestic Volcán de Fuego rises to a picture-perfect peak crowned by a wisp of smoke. This is an area of spectacular beauty, full of birds and native wildlife. A 5,000-acre estate, the property now operates partly as a hotel and partly as a working ranch growing organic coffee and vegetables. It is owned and run by a dedicated branch of the family of the late British financier Sir James Goldsmith, who are keen to continue his ecological ambitions for the region.

Built between 1879 and 1890 by Arnoldo Vogel, a German immigrant, the original house with its neoclassical chapel was expanded by Sir James to 60,000 square feet. His architect, Robert Couturier, a Frenchman living in New York, had to rebuild the hacienda, as it was swamped by jungle and roofless in parts. Today the manicured gardens have the feeling of a leisurely country estate, and the new central courtyard is filled with grapefruit and orange trees. The original entry courtyard contains a traditional Spanish formal garden in which tiled paths, edged with low hedges, radiate from a star-shaped central fountain.

Couturier restored the main guest wing of the hacienda, which opens onto a plant-filled courtyard with a large carved stone fountain. A ground-floor passage is lined with Mexican urns and potted palms.

Water can be seen everywhere throughout the property, flowing along the original Roman-style aqueduct built of volcanic stone, then descending to fountains and rills that playfully crisscross and punctuate the gardens, before symbolically arriving at the giant-sized swimming pool that Couturier placed at the bottom of the garden. Here one sees the postcard view of the volcano, which on most days emits a sometimes unsettling stream of vapor.

Spaces throughout the hacienda have been put to good use: the roof is now a terrace, with spectacular views over the surrounding forest, which echoes with the sounds of bird calls. The interiors of the house are traditional Mexican, richly decorated with antiques and crafts found in nearby Guadalajara and in craft markets all over Mexico.

Local volcanic stone was used throughout the building—for floors, steps, and fireplaces. A small amphitheater, carved out of the sloping garden, has seating fashioned from the porous black stone.

For the adventurous, walks and horseback trails wind through the surrounding forests, leading to picturesque groves of giant bamboo, lakes, and endless opportunities for picnicking.

Like most haciendas, San Antonio has a serene feeling of isolation, with the added patrician resemblance to the European estate of a minor royal, accentuated by its grand facades, its formal garden, and its carefully planned water courses. James Goldsmith was a consummate European, part English and part French, and his former country residence very much reflects this.

His daughter, Alix Marcaccini, and her Italian husband, Goffredo, have redeveloped and furnished San Antonio as a hotel. They are carrying on the family tradition of hospitality with a new ecological twist at the hacienda, giving visitors a chance to discover the great natural beauty of this remote but accessible part of Mexico.

■ A pair of hacienda horses with traditional Mexican saddles wait in front of the main entrance.

■ CLOCKWISE FROM ABOVE: The main dining room has a vaulted brick ceiling and tropical murals. From their rooms, guests have a spectacular view of the volcano. A roof terrace leads to a media room. The swimming pool is placed unobtrusively, at the bottom of the garden. An ornamental candelabra illuminates a hallway.

"I WAS DRIVING THROUGH THE COUNTRYSIDE and I couldn't believe what I was seeing," says designer Jorge Almada. "Off to the distance, in the middle of nowhere, was what looked like a series of towers in the empty flat landscape." He had been driving for several hours across rural landscapes with only occasional green patches of irrigation to relieve the dry desert expanses of cactus and brush, and was ready to believe it was a mirage.

HACIENDA DE
JARAL DE BERRIO

■ The formal upstairs rooms retain their melancholy atmosphere. They form an enfilade across the front of the 19th-century addition.

In search of a craftsman for a furniture project, Almada was traveling with Anne-Marie Midy, his partner in Casa Midy, the design company based in San Miguel de Allende. Before they moved to Mexico, they had lived together in New York—the home of the skyscraper—but they were still unprepared for the dramatic appearance of this group of buildings that had popped up in the desert.

They decided to investigate, and they eventually found themselves in a cloud of dust at the majestic nineteenth-century facade of the former Hacienda de Jaral de Berrio. Vividly incongruous, as haciendas often are, it sits like a grand ruined opera house overlooking a large dirt square filled with tall conical storehouses and two large churches. It doesn't seem to belong at all in its rural surroundings, with its ornate exterior and magnificent upper-floor gallery open to the winds. From the road one can peer through the large windows and see traces of elaborate wallpaper—stripped and peeling, but still compellingly beautiful.

To the left are the remains of a much older hacienda, built with the thick adobe walls of the seventeenth century, that extend

The upstairs rooms open onto a two-story courtyard. Remains of previous wallpaper can be seen where an inner structure has been removed; numerous combinations of vibrant 19th-century wallpaper can still be found at the hacienda.

the property along one side of the village square. Built as a mescal-producing farm, it is the flamboyant nineteenth-century wing, with the sparkling surface of detailed wallpapers, that is evidence of the much greater prosperity during this period.

Almada persuaded a watchman to open the large entry doors, revealing a grassy open courtyard. To his amazement, he discovered a vast decaying ballroom with grand French windows opening onto the street, now barred and shuttered. However, even in the gloom it was still possible to make out ornate friezes and wallpaper details with elaborate crown moldings cut out in fretwork.

As he explored further along arcaded walkways, Almada discovered that the rooms opening onto the central courtyard were mostly closed up, although he could peer through cracks to see one ghostly interior after another. The most magnificent spaces, however, were up on the next floor, reached by a grand staircase, with large arched broken windows defined by worn-away moldings in papier-mâché and roofed with a central cupola. Almada found an almost Byzantine chapel, with empty arches at one end of a sumptuously ornamented room. Its broken skylight cast an ethereal glow. Its elaborate walls had been nonetheless quite well preserved in the near darkness.

Almada found room after room covered in nineteenth-century wallpaper, hand painted, some printed. These formal rooms seemed melancholy, stripped of furniture, door trims, fireplaces, and flooring, but had a particular sense of enchantment.

"Some people don't understand its beauty, they find it sad," says Almada, who has returned several times, "but Anne-Marie and I find it compelling. We picnic in the central courtyard and spend the day roaming the almost one hundred rooms of the hacienda."

When Almada returned to San Miguel he found that a local architect, Roberto Burillo, was in charge of the restoration of Jaral de Berrio, and had researched the history of the vast house and why it was abandoned. Burillo explained that the hacienda was once a tremendous estate stretching from the state of Hidalgo to San Luis Potosi. Once a railroad was built over by the highway, mescal and produce were shipped out to the rest of the distant world by their own train service.

The residential history of the Jaral valley dates from 1592, when the first Spanish settlers defended themselves against the war-like Chichimeca tribe that lived in the region, so it wasn't until the eighteenth century that the hacienda was in full swing. The de Berrio family, who had taken over the large estate by marriage, owned nearly one hundred haciendas, making them one of the largest property owners in New Spain. At that time the lands must have comprised an estate as big as a small country; the Hacienda de Jaral de Berrio was considered its capital.

In the nineteenth century it reached its peak of prosperity, and the main wing was added, with all its Victorian detail. In 1855 nearly 7,000 people lived in and around the huge estate.

But time took its toll, and the land was broken up, and eventually the local council, or *ejido*, took ownership of the main buildings. Sadly, it had been neglected since the 1950s. Recently, however, a group of Mexico City businessmen bought the building and the nearby mescal factory, and with the help of Burillo, is slowly bringing the property back to life.

"We are already selling a small amount of mescal made in the hacienda's factories," Burillo says, talking about his plans for the future. "And when finances permit, we will continue the restoration. Right now our goal is to get the buildings as structurally sound as possible." So the Hacienda de Jaral de Berrio will remain a poetic ruin for a few years before it is finally restored to its former glory.

HACIENDA ARANJUEZ

ARTISTS HAVE TRADITIONALLY BEEN DRAWN to Mexico, as art is the heart and soul of the country, expressed by the colors and drama of everyday Mexican life.

The rich traditions of craftsmanship here have inspired many artists and sculptors, and in this spirit about ten years ago artist James Brown moved to Oaxaca with his wife, Alexandra, and their three children. They followed in the footsteps of James's brother Matthew, who had already set up rug-weaving production in nearby Teotitlán del Valle to manufacture the designs of a growing list of international artists.

The Browns fell in love with Oaxaca's otherworldly atmosphere. Located in a valley surrounded by the remote mountains of southwestern Mexico, it is an important center of indigenous crafts, a beautiful and historic city with the important Aztec ruins of Mitla and Monte Albán a short drive away. It is also an art center linked with the names of some of Mexico's most famous twentieth-century artists. The beautiful Rufino Tamayo Museum, which houses

■ A dog rests peacefully under the vaulted roof of the original 18th-century entrance to the hacienda.

that artist's own collection of pre-Hispanic artifacts, is located in the center of town.

The Browns discovered the seventeenth-century Hacienda Aranjuez in the foothills just outside Oaxaca. The property was once extensive enough to have provided food for the nearby Convent of Santo Domingo. Trails lead from here up into the mountains on one side, and the city is a five-minute drive on the other, visible as a ribbon of twinkling lights at night.

Visitors arrive in an arcaded entry courtyard. As with all haciendas, the living rooms are endowed with lofty ceilings. The family lives on one side of the hacienda, while the other side gives James plenty of raw studio space. The Browns live as artists in the same

A tiled Mexican bench sits in the garden at the back of the hacienda. Majestic old trees and fountains add to the unmistakable charm of the property.

A small local table filled with books anchors the living area of the hacienda. Colorful red chairs and a small table lead the way to the living room. The courtyard, with its cooling central fountain, separates Brown's studio from the residential part of the hacienda.

■ The Browns designed the four-poster iron bed. A 17th-century French tapestry hangs on the wall.

bohemian style, casual and improvised, that they have adopted in their other homes in New York, Paris, and Greece.

The living room is furnished simply and colorfully. The dining room has a vaulted ceiling and yellow painted chairs and table, which like most of the furniture has been made by local artisans to the Browns' specifications. "We provided them with drawings of the furniture we needed," Alexandra explains, "based on local classical styles, trying to use as simple forms as possible. We did not bring a single piece of furniture from New York."

The master bedroom is dominated by a large iron four-poster bed, also designed by the Browns and made locally, which would probably look enormous anywhere else. There is little else in the room, emphasizing its generous space. They brought the seventeenth-century tapestry from France. From here, doors open onto a broad arcaded loggia overlooking a rustic fountain set in a landscape of wild grasses, with pastures beyond.

James Brown uses half of the hacienda as his painting studio. Here a work in progress sits for viewing on a long bench.

HACIENDAS
OF THE YUCATÁN

The Basilica of San Antonio de Padua overlooks the town of Izamal.

THE YUCATÁN PENINSULA IS SCATTERED WITH thousands of haciendas, some beautifully restored, others still roofless picturesque ruins, overgrown by creepers and waiting to be brought back to life again.

Many of these beautiful buildings, dating from the days of the first Spanish colonization, are slumbering away in the jungle. They were originally built as an effective means of controlling the large native population, but they flourished because they were also incredibly prosperous, at least before the Second World War.

In Mayan times, sisal, called *ci*, was used for clothing and even pounded into a restorative drink for the hot climate of the Yucatán. But it wasn't until the nineteenth century that the area began producing sisal in earnest. The invention of the McCormick corn harvester in the United States fueled the explosive growth of the industry, as the harvester needed sisal rope to bind the harvested crops.

Haciendas always had a chapel or church; this is a fine neoclassical example. An arched walkway along the front of the Basilica of San Antonio de Padua in Izamal.

Also called henequen, sisal is an agave-type plant with long fleshy leaves, not unlike the agave used to make tequila. The leaves were harvested and then stripped by steam-driven or diesel mill equipment, dried on racks, and then shipped by local railway, often owned by the haciendas themselves, to the port towns of Sisal and Progreso. The raw plant eventually became a strong fiber that was mainly used for rope and string before the invention of nylon.

Large areas of land were already in use for cattle ranches, maize, and sugar cane, so it was not difficult for the haciendas to change track and grow the new crop instead. These estates took over an amazing 60 percent of the Yucatán peninsula. However, to process this crop the rancher needed factories to house the equipment. These *haciendados* were often sophisticated and well-traveled men who took this on as a design challenge, and the factories were built to blend in with the traditional hacienda architecture, which often included elements from Greek and Roman classical architecture as well as the equally well-proportioned and harmonious traditional Spanish colonial style.

When the international demand for sisal dropped after the end of the Second World War, the hacienda owners eventually relinquished their estates, which became deserted ruins slowly returning to the jungle. It took nearly sixty years for these national treasures to be rediscovered, and now they form a chain of small hotels and private country houses across the peninsula, sensitively restored, where the beauty and splendor of the Yucatán can be appreciated in the comfort and style of the historic old land barons of Mexico.

The impressive entry gates to the Hacienda Temozon, in the Yucatán. The original hacienda was built in the 17th century.

HACIENDA UAYAMON

AS YOU DRIVE UP TO THE MAIN SQUARE OF THE Hacienda Uayamon and peer through a small thicket of trees, you can still see traces of the original majesty of the impressive estate. To the right of the main house is an artful composition of beautiful old stone walls and arches that are now romantically lit by night. These walls are part of the vast ruins of the sisal production factories that brought such riches to the hacienda in the nineteenth century.

Nonetheless, Uayamon is one of the Yucatán's oldest haciendas, dating to long before its sisal-producing days. Part of the district of Campeche, it was built in colonial times by the Spanish as a cattle farm. By the nineteenth century Uayamon was as busy as a small town, growing cattle, corn, sugar cane, and the new crop, sisal. Its own railway was built around 1904 to ship its produce out of the area, and by 1908 the tracks reached as far as Campeche.

Uayamon is now a hotel, one of a series of successfully converted haciendas strung across the Yucatán peninsula. The twentieth-century restoration has preserved the atmosphere of faded grandeur. Buried within the ancient stone walls is a long swimming pool designed by architect Salvador Reyes Rios; rising from the water is a pair of old columns from the original complex that gives the site the feel of a magnificent Roman bath. The chapel has simply been

■ The beautiful ruined arches of the old sisal factory are lit at night. Caballeros wait with their horses in front of the stone walls.

swept and left roofless and unrestored, but it still exudes a religious aura of calm and peace from within its slowly crumbling walls.

The majestic ceiba (or kapok) tree—really two trees grown together—to the right of the main building is more than a hundred years old and it is a local landmark with its own legend. Tradition warns that a drunken man who leans against the tree during the full moon is in grave danger of being confronted by a red-headed woman with rooster feet. She will spirit him away and he will never be seen again.

■ An imposing staircase leads up to the main house and its terrace. The swimming pool was built in the old sisal factory, incorporating a pair of old columns from the original structure.

A small water tank in front of the main hacienda building has been turned into a lily pond, acting as natural air conditioning in the tropical heat. The old well still remains near the main house; troughs and wells are recycled as dramatic accents on the property.

THIS BAROQUE RUIN OF A HACIENDA SHOWS that even in decay, these ancient buildings can still be things of magic and beauty. Not far from Campeche, San José Carpizo was built in the Mexican neoclassical style that was popular around the turn of

HACIENDA
SAN JOSÉ CARPIZO

the century. The crumbling sisal factory, main house, workshops, church, and other hacienda buildings edge a large plaza, which has now become a deserted and dusty children's playground. Just visible on the front facade of each building is its title, signifying its previous place in the scheme of things. The clearly marked "Talleria" is now being reused as the village shop, while other structures, picturesquely ruined, are used for storage and living quarters by the local villagers.

The hacienda and its buildings have been taken over by the villagers, who are letting the jungle reclaim the rest. The chapel, however, is still loved and well patronized; its interior details are intact and decorated according to the seasons and festivals of the Church. Each simple seat bears the name of the family that provided it.

■ The original chapel of the hacienda is still being used by the village. Simple whitewashed benches contrast with the ornately stenciled walls. The altar is framed by trompe l'oeil ocher curtains and plaster swags and tassels.

Original paneled stenciling enlivens the walls, and theatrical painted curtains frame the altar.

The main house is in ruins, but some idea of its past glory can still be seen. Traces of friezes run along the exposed walls, and the main facade still bears the original decorative tiles and proudly displays the year 1910, the date of its construction. Signs of an original garden can still be made out behind the crumbling walls, the height of which gives an idea of its former size, and tall trees grow unchecked, often inside the house itself. Meanwhile, dogs bark in the background, the old wild garden echoes with bird calls, and yellow butterflies flit through the open rooms.

■ The hacienda's whitewashed main office building overlooks the town square. The ruined front facade of the principal hacienda building retains its imported blue tiles, if not its roof.

HACIENDA
SANTA ROSA DE LIMA

HACIENDAS SUCH AS SANTA ROSA DE LIMA have a way of appearing, like a mirage, at the end of a long, dusty, and sometimes mysterious drive, with few encouraging clues along the journey to give any idea of what to expect. Turning off the highway between Campeche and Mérida, you take a series of mazelike country roads that lead eventually through a small village of what were once workers' cottages before suddenly arriving at the patrician gates of this large Yucatecan estate. Then, at last, you see the grand cobble and grass forecourt, the welcoming facade, a stately *casa principal*, and the promise of a tamarindo margarita.

Near the ancient Mayan center of Chunchucmil, which controlled the salt industry, the Spanish conquerors came ashore and seized the land that, after passing through several revolutions and centuries, has now become the peaceful hacienda called Santa Rosa de Lima.

Once a cattle ranch, like most of the old haciendas, this graceful estate adapted to the times and was rebuilt in 1909 as a successful sisal plantation. From here it was a short journey to the port of Sisal, on the coast, from where steamboats shipped the fibers to New Orleans.

The main house, with its well-proportioned colonnades, sits back from a large grassy square with a sense of confident prosperity. On one side is a small chapel painted a warm ocher with bright white trim, while on the other side of the square the old factory buildings, built in 1916, are veiled by thick tropical plantings. The factory chimney still carries the initials H.F.G., after the Fajardo

■ The small red hacienda chapel, dating from the main renovation in 1909, overlooks the garden. OPPOSITE: One of the guest bedrooms holds a pair of twin iron beds; the walls and frieze echo the colors of the Mexican tiled floor.

■ The chimney of the original sisal factory still stands over an entry to the guest rooms. A swimming pool using the original cistern flows through the arches of the bath house above. The front terrace overlooks the main hacienda plaza.

brothers, who formed a partnership to grow the new crop in the early twentieth century.

Hacienda Santa Rosa was opened as a hotel in 1997 after two years of restoration; it now reveals its original splendor. The factory was adapted into rooms and suites, and a swimming pool was set into lawns to the rear. Another pool was created out of the hacienda's original cistern. This flows through brightly painted arches beneath the adjoining bath house. Its drainage is cleverly used to irrigate botanical gardens beyond. These have been planted with a variety of plants used by the Mayans for medicinal purposes.

The main hacienda building is called the *casa principal*, as it usually has the main view over the central plaza. Here it is painted blue with an arcade defined in white, topped with an exterior plaster frieze picked out in red and yellow. Inside, traces of the original friezes at ceiling and chair height have been restored. Glass bell lamps hang from high, beamed ceilings illuminating the tables and wicker chairs of the restaurant. Outside, the broad front terrace is set with comfortable rocking chairs for serene views out across the estate, where the plantation's peacocks stroll past. Beautifully worn red terracotta floor tiles line the passage to the bedrooms, which are bright and airy with high ceilings. Here simple white enameled metal beds made with crisp white linens make a snappy contrast with the red and white tiled floor and the red dado and frieze that runs around the bedroom walls.

Behind the *casa principal* is a large walled tropical garden with vine-covered fruit trees shading paths that wind around the lush plantings and a small inviting terrace furnished with a breakfast table.

Sitting on a comfortable chair on the front terrace, under the spell of the peacocks flirting and fanning through the garden at dusk, it is easy to understand the appeal of the isolated but gracious way of life of the *hacendados* at Santa Rosa.

■ The front terrace is decorated with a frieze of shell motifs running high along the walls near the beamed ceiling. In the restaurant, glass bell lamps hang from the ceiling to illuminate the tables and wicker chairs.

WHEN YOU ARE IN THE VICINITY OF THE HACIENDA Temozon, you know you are in a very special place. This region is full of Mayan ruins, and the hacienda is located on the trail of the Ruta Puuc, which refers to the predominant style of Mayan archi-

HACIENDA TEMOZON

tecture of square-cut blocks found in this part of the Yucatán, at sites like nearby Uxmal, Labna, and Edzna.

This majestic building was first built in 1665 as the estancia of Diego de Mendoza, a descendent of the conquistador Francisco de Montejo. At first producing cattle and maize, the plantation was then transformed into a prosperous sisal business in the late nineteenth century. At this stage it had an area of over 16,000 acres, more than 640 workers, and boasted the most powerful industrial equipment in the region. With the beginning of the twentieth century and increased prosperity, the hacienda was expanded and the

A cool dining terrace overlooks the garden. Perforated wood trim fills the rounded arches of the open windows.

The red pigmented walls of the hacienda are the original color. The impressive entry gates have been repainted and restored. The swimming pool leads into a rill of water in the Spanish style.

gardens were redesigned, only to fall victim to land reform in 1917, when it was reduced to half its size.

The entrance to the Hacienda Temozon is designed to impress. Formal gardens lead to low, well-proportioned stairways, past a row of dolphin-head fountains that flank the steps, greeting visitors as they proceed to the large terrace of the main house. From a loggia at the *casa principal* you can overlook the expanse of well-kept garden in front of the property.

Temozon was restored and opened as a hotel in 1997 using the materials of the turn of the century, including the red, yellow,

The main steps are flanked by rows of dolphin-head fountains and lead up to the main house. A 19th-century carriage sits in the covered veranda of the old hacienda factory, kept cool by rows of ceiling fans.

and blue mineral pigments that once again decorate its walls and architectural features.

The old sisal factory has been restored to give an idea of how the fiber was processed, and some of the original machinery is still set up in the massive open spaces of the industrial building.

This now ornaments a peaceful and beautiful garden that also has what is probably the largest swimming pool in the Yucatán. Six tall columns architecturally articulate this big stretch of water leading from the main house. Water, an important element in this hot climate, is used architecturally in the hacienda garden for both practical and visual reasons.

A high-ceilinged guest bedroom is cooled by fans. The bentwood curves of the cane-seated bench echo the wrought-iron detailing of the double bed. The original hammock hooks are still set into the wall. The bathrooms have built-in marbletop washbasins.

HACIENDA KATANCHEL

IT IS SOMETHING OF A MIRACLE THAT THE Hacienda Katanchel still stands just outside Mérida on the road to Izamal. It has survived revolution, dereliction, and then, in 2002, Hurricane Isidore, which battered the hacienda for twelve hours. "It stopped above Katanchel after it had hit Cuba," explains owner Monica Hernandez, "trapped by a cold front that couldn't move on because of the hurricane. So it stayed where it was, directly above us."

The predominantly nineteenth-century Hacienda Katanchel had been beautifully restored by the Spanish architect Anibal Gonzalez and his Mexican wife, Monica Hernandez, and opened to the public as a hotel for only three years when tragedy struck. Now after three more years of repairs, it is restored again but is no longer a hotel. The couple use it for entertaining their friends and for weekend visits.

Katanchel is approached by a dead straight two-and-a-half-mile lane that is so narrow that that the hedges often brush against the car on both sides. Finally an imposing gateway announces the hacienda. The red buildings of Katanchel are set in 740 acres of jungle, gardens, and Mayan ruins hidden in the vegetation. An

■ An antique Mexican sideboard is decorated with blue and white Mexican pottery topped by glass pulque balls. OPPOSITE: In the hacienda's *sala principal*, elaborate 19th-century painted friezes are still apparent.

casa mexicana style ▐ **139**

original tramline, once used to transport the sisal, still circles the property, and trams pulled by a donkey transport hotel guests to their cottages.

Anibal and Monica decided to focus on reforestation and restoring the ecology of the area. The property is largely self-sufficient: most of the vegetables and fruit are grown on the estate, which has its own water source from deep wells. Water is pumped by windmills through irrigation channels to the swimming pool and throughout the hacienda. The swimming pool is drained weekly, cleaned, and refilled with fresh spring water. Water from the taps is potable.

When the couple bought the crumbling hacienda it was in ruins, with trees growing through roofless buildings. Anibal undertook the architectural challenge to restore it and to reinvent the spaces into organized living areas. There were also historic requirements to consider, as Katanchel was once the site of a Mayan observatory.

The arched front entrance of the hacienda retains original painted details inside. The walls that surround the hacienda are painted the same color as the buildings, and trimmed in white. An oriental rug is hung on the back wall of the entrance.

■ The 19th-century-style billiard room. Its stenciled arch and vibrant tiled floor create a rich and lively atmosphere.

A yellow and white guest bedroom has a high ceiling, and a wrought-iron bed with jaunty metal pennants. The wall color, made with local yellow minerals, is called "amarillo Izamal" after a nearby town. These guest rooms have witty and charming beds designed by Anibal Gonzalez.

So, to stay out of trouble, they were very careful not to disturb the grounds and keep to the layout of the original property.

Deciding at that point to open Katanchel as a hotel, the couple added thirty-three suites as separate buildings, all laid out along well-kept paths on the grounds, following the route of the tram. Then Monica swept in with her plantings and cleverly hid the cottages with tropical landscaping.

The entry building still has beautifully stenciled walls from the nineteenth century, next to a little chapel with black-and-white marble floors imported from Italy. The tiled floors here and throughout the hacienda are made in the Yucatán, and the wall color is a Mayan yellow made with local minerals, called "amarillo Izamal," after the nearby yellow-painted town of Izamal.

The former sisal factory has become a dramatic series of rooms of Victorian splendor. The main area has a soaring ceiling, forming a magnificent sitting room, and it opens onto an adjoining billiard salon painted a cheerful yellow.

The hotel became a huge success, and its food was praised by magazines all over the world. It was constantly filled with interesting guests who were attracted to the Yucatán by the culture, avian life, and Mayan ruins. Even though it has been restored to private use, the owners sometimes rent the hacienda for special events.

The couple love this often dramatic part of Mexico. Monica grew up near here, in a hacienda in Veracruz further up the coast, where she had a wonderful rural childhood; as a result she is passionately committed to the ecology of the area.

Sisal, explains Monica, "was an ecological disaster for the Yucatán, as the land had to be totally cleared to plant it." Her lifetime goal is to help restore the local landscape to its original richness and diversity.

■ Two guests are given a tour of the hacienda in a donkey-pulled tram car on rails, the old method of transporting sisal from the factory. A simple metal table and chairs are ready for afternoon tea.

HACIENDA PUERTA CAMPECHE IS NOT STRICTLY a hacienda, but it has the same atmosphere, charm, and distinctive rural style as its more authentic cousins. Created out of a small cluster of decayed and roofless eighteenth-century town houses

HACIENDA PUERTA CAMPECHE

in the middle of the colorful coastal town of Campeche, the hotel has the feel of a hacienda's rambling spaces, is surrounded by history, and protected by the ancient fortified city wall that circles the town.

The houses have undergone a process similar to the rehabilitation of ruined haciendas, and consequently have been beautifully restored as hotel suites. The pièce de résistance is the central pool. This has been conceptually designed to flow in and out of one of the old ruined houses to give bathers the surreal experience of exploring the property by swimming through it, or simply enjoying the space from one of the hammocks suspended across the water.

Campeche, which is a UNESCO World Heritage site and still filled with sixteenth-century buildings, is a town to be explored on foot. This and visiting the nearby Mayan ruins and pre-Columbian museum are the main attractions for guests here, and Hacienda Puerta Campeche is perfectly placed to explore this lesser-known end of the Yucatán peninsula.

One of the original ruins has been converted into a swimming pool in the center of the building. Steps lead down to the shallow pool, which flows through many of the old rooms.

An old tree clings to the wall of the central hotel courtyard. Outdoors and indoors, the pools create a cooling, restful atmosphere, with hammocks ready for a siesta over the water.

The Mexican coast seems like paradise to the visitor from cold northern climates. Palm trees sway over broad, sandy beaches inspiring relaxation, and the sparkling water is always warm. On one side of the continent Mexico meets the Caribbean, while on the other it stretches along the edge of the Pacific, around the Sea of Cortez, and meanders around numerous small bays and inlets on the way.

HOUSES BY THE SEA

There are many different ways of building a beach house in Mexico, but most borrow from local indigenous architecture that evolved over centuries to make the most of shade and cool breezes. Thatch-roofed houses called *palapas* are the basic building units here. These elegant structures have evolved to their grandest scale in communities such as Careyes, on the Pacific coast south of Puerto Vallarta.

Of course other types of architecture can also be found along the coast of Mexico. Fishing villages dense with small brightly painted houses are cheerful and lively places to stay if you are looking for sun and warm weather, while a large majestic villa with domes and arches dramatically overlooking a rugged patch of coast can be as elegant as a fine mansion anywhere in the world. The variety of housing is endless.

Here we show houses along the Pacific coast by Marco Aldaco and Enrique Zozaya, both large (Cuixmala) and small (Casa Tortuga in Baja California).

Manolo Mestre has also designed many houses along the coast from Acapulco to Puerto Vallarta, but most of them are near Careyes, where he has brought his sense of careful positioning to each house. Duccio Ermenegildo's courtyard home in Careyes is inland, with just a rooftop view of the ocean.

As elegant and exotic as these coastal houses are, their most evocative signature is a casually slung hammock, with as many pillows as possible.

■ CLOCKWISE FROM ABOVE: A thatched-roof beach house in Acapulco by Marco Aldaco. Dinner preparation in a kitchen designed by Duccio Ermenegildo. The blue painted terrace looks out to the sea at Careyes. A signature curved staircase by Manolo Mestre.

LA META

ALTHOUGH ARTIST MARI CARMEN HERNANDEZ moved to Paris many years ago from her native Mexico, she has never lost touch with her origins. Slim and graceful, with long, striking gray hair, she was a close friend of architect Luis Barragán, and left Mexico for Paris when she realized she was not destined to be an architect. Nonetheless, Mexico has always been the source of her inspiration, and with that in mind, she decided to create a summer house and studio for herself and her son on Mexico's Pacific coast.

■ Simple built-in wooden benches surround the granite-topped table in the dining area; Hernandez's painting is in the background. OPPOSITE: The lap pool tapers in a stagelike illusion of length. The rope swing makes a good diving board.

Sheltered by the thatched palapa roof, the orange-pink adobe staircase embraces the front of the house, concealed on the facade by a curving wall. At its top are the main bedroom and studio.

Working with Mexican architect Enrique Zozaya, she found the perfect site in Troncones, a community on a long sandy beach just north of the resort town of Ixtapa. Here they designed a house with plenty of space for a studio, her family, and friends, surrounded by pink bougainvillea and the ocean. Additional design ideas came from her friend Duccio Ermenegildo, also an architect and the designer of several homes in Careyes.

After a long ride along the coast road from Ixtapa it is a relief to arrive at the picturesque entry to La Meta, which opens into a large cobbled courtyard. A path leads to the house, with its welcoming two-storied facade of faded pink-orange walls topped with a roof

Natural building materials and finishings were used in the artist's studio. The efficient kitchen has built-in seating and overhead plate racks against its adobe walls. Sand dollars found on the beach have a sculptural appeal.

of palm thatch. To the left of the entry the organic curve of an adobe staircase leads to an open upstairs mezzanine area, where Hernandez has hung a row of vividly colored Mexican hammocks. Her own rooms lie beyond this, a magnificent studio with an open bedroom that looks out to the ocean. To one side a small balcony presents a view of palm trees and the thatched roofs of the neighboring houses. In the studio she is currently working on a painting in her series *Moines* (monks) for an exhibition in Paris.

The main floor of La Meta unfolds behind a sculptural screen. The living and dining rooms, with their high ceilings, are completely open to the breezes. The Pacific Ocean is visible and close, seemingly kept at a distance by a long blue and white lap pool that reaches out toward the waves, framed by a tall trellis and a hanging swing. Hernandez, a serious swimmer, wanted a lap pool, but at that point in the construction her land was only twenty meters wide. The solution was to build using a false perspective—the pool narrows as it heads toward the beach, providing the illusion of width. She has since bought more land and has now planted an oasis of palm trees to add to the tropical view from the house.

The entry gate is covered in bougainvillea; steps between two thatched outbuildings lead to the main house. A small balcony off the master bedroom. A casual bench on the way to the beach.

A plainly finished wall behind the rough-cut granite dining table provides a place for Hernandez to hang her paintings, which are influenced by nature and by Mexico.

Much of the furniture in the house is built into the architecture. Organic continuations of the walls form bed bases, benches, side tables, and even bathtubs. When Hernandez arrives from Paris, all she has to do is add cushions, benches, and small wooden tables to make the house complete.

CASA TORTUGA

IN THE LAST TWO DECADES CABO SAN LUCAS has been transformed from a somewhat primitive beach and fishing resort into a real-estate bonanza. The highway from the newly rebuilt Los Cabos airport is now lined with some of the world's most glamorous resorts and a succession of improbable-looking golf courses set in the arid desert landscape. Whereas a few years ago a sprinkling of houses and an occasional hotel competed only with cactus along this dramatically stark coastline, the same oceanfront today has an almost urban density, with remaining lots approaching Malibu-like price levels.

Alison Palevsky's beach house, Casa Tortuga, is perched on rocks at the water's edge just minutes from the bustling town of Cabo San Lucas, with sweeping views of the ocean and the parade of fishing boats setting out early in the morning in search of game fish. It is a house where the rhythmic sound of the ocean is constantly present. There is a small terrace in front of the house for sunbathing and cooling off in a little pool, and an upper terrace, also facing the view, for dining. Compact as the house is, there are several guest rooms, each decorated quite simply.

■ Curved steps lead into the organic stucco house. Agave plants in Mexican pots make strong silhouettes against the textured white walls.

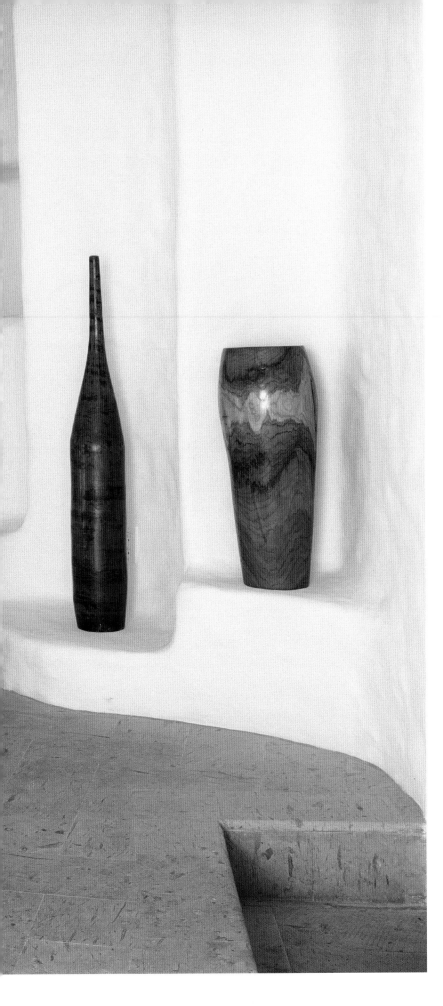

■ Upstairs, the organic
walls provide seating
areas and bases for
elegant wood vases. The
organic bathtub is lit by a
skylight and a pair of tall
beeswax candles.

The house is part of a dense residential enclave between the ocean and the main coastal highway. Steps lead from a tiny street down to the entry door, which gives little hint of the house's dramatic living spaces within and the imminence of the ocean suddenly glimpsed (and heard) outside the windows. A small vestibule leads directly into an organically designed main living room defined by a perforated inner wall edged with built-in banquettes. These surround a lofty central domed space with a soaring skylight. Around this inner core, circulation routes radiate to oceanfront terraces and guest rooms.

The house was designed as a weekend retreat by Palevsky and her design partner, Sarah Shetter, as an escape from the designer's busy life in Los Angeles. Cabo San Lucas is only ninety minutes by plane from Los Angeles, and it is very simple for Alison, her family, and her friends to breeze into her beach house for weekends. What a reward for such a short commute: waking up to the sounds of the ocean and a breathtaking view of the arches of Land's End, the dramatic rock formation to which Cabo owes so much of its fame.

■ The terrace overlooks the ocean, and its small swimming pool faces where the Sea of Cortez meets the Pacific. The terrace railing is made of peeled wood tied with rope. A similar design was created for the bed, which is suspended from the ceiling; its striking combination of wood, rope, and mosquito netting gives it a romantic and poetic quality.

WHEN YOU ARRIVE AT THE PUERTO VALLARTA airport you are immediately hit by a blast of tropical air. Even the airport looks beautiful; surrounded by coconut palms, it has a raffish tropical charm. The Punta Mita estate is only a twenty-minute drive up the coast. At its center is the luxurious Four Seasons Hotel, which is surrounded by gracious private estates that fringe this broad bay. The video entrepreneur Joe Francis, who is based in Los Angeles, has a new house here that is just large enough to accommodate the creative energies of his designer, Martyn Lawrence-Bullard.

CASA ARAMARA

■ The entry to the Casa Aramara has a clear view of the ocean. OPPOSITE: Hand-colored raffia balls hang dramatically from the thatched dining room ceiling.

This was a huge project for Martynus-Tripp, a small but very successful design company based in Los Angeles. At 40,000 square feet the home was a challenge to furnish, and Lawrence-Bullard's design partner, Trip Haenisch, had to organize a shipload of furniture, specifically designed for each room, from as far away as Indonesia.

Pathways lined with tropical plantings lead to a broad entry with a small central fountain inset into the floor. From here passages and flights of stairs lead to guest quarters, spas, and the private regions of the house, as well as offer a tempting glimpse of a huge palapa-roofed living room and the ocean beyond. This is a house designed for entertaining, and Francis customarily arrives for weekends with an entourage of houseguests. He is an unusually dedicated host. Resort services include round-the-clock bedside massages, saunas, scuba diving, water skiing, and tennis.

Lawrence-Bullard has tried to infuse intimacy and idiosyncratic detail into a weekend house that is resortlike in scale. In the dining room at one end of the living space, for example, a massive table overhung with festive lighting is anchored and made more personable by a glass-fronted cabinet displaying collections of seashells that seem to have been collected over a lifetime.

Haenisch designed the dining table out of one huge piece of wood and shipped it to Mexico, but he had to hire twenty people to bring it into the house. This is definitely living on a large scale.

■ A bench upholstered in Indonesian blue batik sits below a row of the author's photographs. The pebbled floor has been laid in a chevron pattern. Martynus-Tripp designed the doors throughout the house; here they have inserts of blue glass in a Moorish design.

COSTA CAREYES

MAGAZINES FROM ALL OVER THE WORLD COME to photograph in Careyes, with page after page of photos showing its interiors, its lifestyle, and its beaches. Not bad for a little town with one hotel and few restaurants that is hours from the nearest airport.

The reason for all this attention is the homogenous—and extremely photogenic—Careyes style of architecture that has evolved over the last thirty-five years on the Pacific coast of Mexico. This

■ A row of saddled horses are groomed while waiting for a game at the local Careyes polo fields. OPPOSITE: Viewed from the ocean, a typical Careyes house is a vivid splash of color in the landscape.

■ The beauty of the
Careyes coast provides
a dramatic view from
most of the beach houses.
The colorful houses of
the Casitas de las Flores
each have a view of the
Playa Rosa.

■ Many beach houses have their best views from the roof. Here an outdoor daybed surrounded by pillows provides a comfortable place to watch the sunset. Gianfranco Brignone, the founder of Careyes, built a studio with a "stairway to heaven."

began with a formative house for Loel and Gloria Guinness in Acapulco, designed by the Guadalajara-based architect Marco Aldaco in the early 1970s, which broke away from the then-conventional modernist air-conditioned box. With its palapa roof and open sides to allow the air to pass through, this house followed an organically shaped plan. Aldaco then designed the first house in Careyes in a similar style for its founder, Gianfranco Brignone. This was adopted as the blueprint for everything that followed, and Brignone, the resort's ongoing developer, has made sure that Careyes enjoys that rare thing in our present-day world: a consistent, homogenous style of architecture.

This Careyes style further evolved from a fusion of indigenous materials and modern design. Aldaco and the other architects working in the town blended local traditions with a more contemporary spatial rigor in the planning of these houses, especially with modern requirements for the kitchens and bathrooms.

With its wild sandy beaches, harbor, and cliffs, houses in Careyes are situated in a variety of settings. The cliff-top houses are the most familiar, each with its palapa roof and sublime infinity-edged pool that hovers over the ocean, blending sky and water as patrolling flights of pelicans drift past at eye level. Playa Rosa, the village within Careyes, overlooks the harbor next to the hotel. Here there are villas that can be rented, giving the best opportunity for a visitor to experience this magical resort.

WHEN ARCHITECT DUCCIO ERMENEGILDO BOUGHT
a quarter-acre lot near the coast in Careyes over ten years ago, he
had no idea how building a house in Mexico would change his life.
He was a business partner in a successful restaurant in Mexico City
and had little interest in architecture. However, he was becoming

CASA COLIBRI

more and more intrigued with the food and culture of Mexico. In
April 1995 he visited Careyes for a weekend, when on a whim he
bought the property and its existing small house, which he is still
working on ten years later. It was this house that turned him into
an architect. He learned as he went along, and he discovered how
much he enjoyed creating shapes and spaces.

The property is long and wedge-shaped and set a block back
from the ocean, which is reached down a steep cliff; there is no
real beach. Ermenegildo had to rework the living spaces, create an
ocean view, and build a spacious kitchen, as he enjoys entertaining
and is an excellent cook.

While the house is not large, what makes it work so well are
the carefully considered spaces between the new structures. The
whole property appears to drift toward the swimming pool, which
is exactly where you want to be in the warm tropical climate of
Careyes.

To camouflage the narrow width of the lot, the entrance to
the house is planted with a woven tunnel of hibiscus, which opens
to a thatched palapa, the main entertaining space. The house, Casa
Colibri, is named after the hummingbirds that flit in between the

■ The main living palapa
at Casa Colibri, seen from
the swimming pool. To
the left is the kitchen,
while the building behind
houses the bedrooms and
Ermenegildo's studio.

■ Views of the house show how Ermenegildo uses color to graphically define Casa Colibri's well-proportioned walls. A Guatemalan hammock, sheltered by a simple lattice, fills the terrace outside his studio.

red hibiscus. From there the garden leads to an open dining room and a thatched-roof kitchen, enigmatically windowless except at the rear of the building, where it opens onto a barbeque area. The kitchen is well laid out and the most recent addition has been a cold storage room, reached through an impressive stainless steel–insulated door.

Careyes owes its charm to a fairly strict building code enforced since the area was developed. However, hidden in the rustic beauty of the adobe walls and thatched roofs of a typical beach building can be found any number of high-tech conveniences. Ermenegildo, for example, has high-speed wireless internet access throughout his property, and satellite television brings programming from all over the world.

Ermenegildo planted the garden with thick walls of palm trees, which also hide the narrow width of the land, so that the house feels set in a forest, especially upstairs, where it is sheltered from the view of the neighboring properties. He built an open living room here to make the most of the only ocean view. Conveniently angled to the west and the setting sun, the large, comfortable sofas where he and his girlfriend, Nicolle Meyer, relax and watch the sunset have the best view from the house. However, not content to keep working on the paradise he has created here, Ermenegildo has accepted other work. He has built another beach house here in Careyes, which was featured in many magazines, and is currently working on a second house in the Dominican Republic, as well as projects in Ibiza and France. This, of course, means more building here in Careyes, as now he needs more studio space: he is working on adding yet another room.

■ The master bath has a private open courtyard. The tub is poured concrete with a top coat of white concrete mixed with marble powder. A chair with a cowhide seat accents the library off the master bedroom.

■ Ermenegildo designed
the furniture in the main
palapa and the upstairs
terrace to be low, in order
to preserve the view of
the pool, the surrounding
tropical garden, and
the ocean.

An accomplished cook, Ermenegildo enjoys entertaining his friends in a trellised pavilion with a table and chairs he designed. The kitchen courtyard is used for food preparation and al fresco meals.

CUIXMALA

■ The Cuixmala riding stables, which echo the traditional hacienda style, were built to house horses for guests and family. OPPOSITE: A dramatic series of steps in the style of old Italian cascades form a backdrop to the main pool area at La Loma, the main house of Cuixmala. PAGES 196–97: A smaller pool overlooks the private beach.

BRITISH BILLIONAIRE FINANCIER SIR JAMES Goldsmith was looking for a private paradise when he bought land on a remote and rugged strip of the Mexican coast in 1987. Twenty years later it has been transformed into an exotic estate, part Xanadu and part ecological preserve.

A few miles south of the beach resort of Careyes, Cuixmala stretches from the coastal highway to the Pacific Ocean. It is a stunning property.

There are 2,000 acres of richly varied terrain: forested hills overlook plantations leading to a savannah-like plain populated with zebras, gazelles, and ocelots, and coastal lagoons teeming with contented native crocodiles. Two miles of secluded beach stretch from

end to end of the property, where thousands of turtles return to breed every year. Cuixmala is set within a 30,000-acre biosphere, presided over by resident biologists, that pioneer-ecologist Goldsmith established together with the University of Mexico to study local flora and fauna. As a result, the estate produces its own supply of organic food.

Working with New York–based architect Robert Couturier, Goldsmith decided to build his own Moorish fantasy house, La Loma, on a bluff above the ocean, surrounding this with houses for his extended family and friends. Some of the houses face the ocean and others look inland to the lagoon. Hidden in the hills behind the valley are riding stables and more houses built for the staff needed for such a large property. True to his environmentalist beliefs, there is no air conditioning at Cuixmala; high ceilings and good air circulation keep interiors cool and fresh.

▨ A shady terrace in La Loma has a comfortable *equipal* bench with striped cushions. The main dining palapa at La Loma, furnished with Indian bone and ebony chairs, has a fabulous view across the entire ecological estate.

■ *Equipal* chairs furnish
some of the many dining
spaces on the property,
their textured brown
surfaces complementing
both natural palettes and
bright painted stucco.
A colorful, light-washed
dining terrace, set with
oversized potted greenery,
is the perfect place for a
sunny, leisurely breakfast.

■ The colorful Casa Arcadia pool house designed by Duccio Ermenegildo has a cement table surrounded by *equipal* dining chairs. Overlooking the pool and with a view of the ocean, it catches cool breezes.

Since his death over ten years ago, Sir James's daughter Alix Marcaccini and her husband, Goffredo, have decided to live there full time, especially as this is a great place to raise their three children, who are avid horse riders. Their own house, Casa Arcadia, sits on a hilltop overlooking the plantation and the ocean. Architect Duccio Ermenegildo has recently been brought in to add a new pool house to Casa Arcadia and a dramatic new pool to another of the guest houses.

■ The Moorish-inspired living room of La Loma has low built-in seating covered with Indian textiles. In a large niche at the back is a Mexican ceramic tree of life. A guest-house bed covered with Mexican fabrics has a view of the property.

All the houses have outdoor terraces designed for relaxing and entertaining groups of friends or families, especially as the property is quite far from towns and restaurants.

The Marcaccinis, who also manage the hotel Hacienda de San Antonio, featured in another chapter, are environmentalists, and they run both properties along strict ecological lines. The natural habitat of the region is kept as intact as possible, and the Cuixmala Ecological Foundation often hosts study groups from universities.

■ Ermenegildo designed this pool at Casa Torre to look out across the property. The Cuixmala estate has many different ecologies. Here family and friends ride horses through a coconut palm plantation.

LAS ALAMANDAS

ISABEL GOLDSMITH HAS DEVELOPED A WILD stretch of the Pacific coast between Careyes and Puerto Vallarta, creating a stunning resort using vivid colors and local Mexican-style architecture. It evolved naturally from her own initial house, built in the 1980s, and expanded into a hotel that has been so successful she has had to move out. She has now built a spectacular house for herself on a headland overlooking the twin bays that form her property.

After a long drive from Puerto Vallarta, it takes a leap of faith to plunge into the jungle along a small dusty road. Just when you start to wonder exactly where you are, a perfectly landscaped

■ A small Mexican serape draped across a Guatemalan hammock in a corner of the main palapa, designed by Manolo Mestre. OPPOSITE: A pink stucco pavilion marks the entry to the beach and one of the hotel's restaurants.

■ A guest-house terrace, designed by Mestre, is furnished with *equipal* chairs around a matching table. Flower petals spell out "bienvenido" on a guestroom bed. PAGES 212–13: The thatched main hotel palapa has a commanding view over the ocean. Circular pebble mosaics in the floor are based on traditional Mexican designs.

driveway appears, leading you to the immaculate and colorful hotel forecourt of Las Alamandas.

The beach is vast, and apart from Goldsmith's new house, which can be spotted above, Las Alamandas is clearly the only property for miles around. The 1,500 acres that surround the hotel form a paradise of exotic trees, palms, and wild birds. It is as if you are in a private nature park.

The fourteen suites are packed full of Mexican furniture and crafts, very comfortable, and create a real Mexican ambiance. The colors of the hotel have been taken from the flowers that carpet the grounds: hot pink bougainvillea, yellow alamandas (hence the name of the hotel), and white gardenias reappear in the pillows, bedspreads, and walls of Las Alamandas. As if to make the point, "bienvenido" is spelled out on every bedspread.

■ This guest-house bedroom, with its coved brick ceiling, was designed by Mestre; its elegant four-poster bed is hung with sheer white cotton curtains. Pathways to the beach and steps to more guest houses meander through the landscape.

■ Poolside palapas and pavilions echo the colors of bougainvillea and yellow alamandas flowers. The property has been a location for many fashion shoots.

CASA LUNA

ONE OF THE GREATEST COMPLIMENTS AN architect can receive when he has completed a building is to get a commission from a neighbor. When Manolo Mestre finished the Casa dos Estrellas on the coast overlooking the Playa Rosa, he got a call from Chris Tribull, who had bought the land next door. Would Mestre build him a house as well?

This was a great chance for Mestre to create a new building that would relate to its neighbor, but assure the optimum privacy for both owners. Since he was already so familiar with the site, he knew exactly how to orient the building toward the best view.

Casa Luna evolved organically, almost as if it shaped itself around the curve of the cliff's edge, overlooking the sea and the horizon beyond. Birds caught in the updraft skim past the pool's edge, which becomes harmoniously part of the natural order. "I wanted to bring the ocean up to the house," explains Mestre, "and we kept the cactus at the pool's edge as it gives depth to the view."

The approach to the property is veiled by a circular entry courtyard, as Mestre directs the visitor quite carefully toward the

An abstract cactus in a red niche gives drama to the main dining room of Casa Luna.

An elegant sweep of the blue swimming pool follows the edge of the cliff. Mestre's love of organic design is seen in his use of stone mosaics, natural fencing, and the preservation of a venerable cactus, left intact at the edge of the pool to create a foreground for the ocean view.

dramatic ocean view. "The round walls with the fountain in the middle act like a filter between the house and the outside world," adds Mestre.

Living spaces are spread out along the length of the property, taking advantage of the ever-present view. They are as open to the elements as possible, as the spirit of Careyes revolves around living outdoors. The dining and living space is set under a shared palapa, while the bedrooms are in a separate wing.

"This house is successful because it is like a form of meditation for Chris every time he visits," Mestre concludes.

A cushion-filled outdoor living room is sheltered by a wooden slat roof. In the entry to the property, gracefully curved walls encircle a fountain cut out of rock; pebble designs echo the geometry of the small courtyard. A vibrant archway links the living areas.

CASA PACIFICA

AT CASA DE CAMPO, A PATRICIAN ENCLAVE IN THE Dominican Republic made famous by Oscar de la Renta, the architectural styles traditionally hover somewhere between Palm Beach and Bermuda, and generally favor colonnaded fronts. When Duccio Ermenegildo finished Casa Pacifica, his house for a local family, the whole town was astonished. They had never seen a Mexican thatched-roof palapa beach house before, especially on such a majestic scale.

Ermenegildo brought to Casa de Campo the same building elements he used in his earlier houses in Careyes, but he added architectural flourishes appropriate for a house of 18,000 square feet. An arcade gives formality to the front facade, and the boldly angled cut in the curved staircase wall can be seen from the entry, with its graphic row of simple wood columns. He arrived with a crew of craftsmen from Careyes to create an authentic Mexican-Pacific vocabulary, particularly with the palapa roofs. The patio floors are made from cement and marble powder, which is hand chiseled when dry to create ridged surfaces that are comfortable to walk on with bare feet and not slippery when wet.

■ The entry to this house has a pebbled courtyard and a central fountain. Ermenegildo introduced this distinctively Mexican style to Casa de Campo.

Palm trees in a patio leading to one of the palapas. A well-equipped outdoor dining area includes a pizza oven. Ermenegildo designed the floor with alternating squares of inset pebbles. In the large open dining room, a curved blue wall with a niche conceals the entry to the kitchen.

The property begins with a high yellow wall and a grandly scaled eighteenth-century Indian entry gate from Jodhpur. Inside, a circular orange-stuccoed courtyard is paved in river rock, which comes from the nearby Rio Chavon, and flanked by palapa-roofed carports. Beyond this, and completing an elegantly composed grouping, are the two main structures, and a space between these leads to the front patio and garden. Before this is reached, a doorway to the right opens into a lofty entry hall with an Ermenegildo-designed and locally made chandelier and a staircase that curves up to the private upstairs quarters.

Facing the ocean, and with neighbors on either side, the house needed privacy. The architect built using a horseshoe plan: two main structures are linked by a continuous paved terrace that curves around an elliptical pool set in an expansive front lawn. Beyond this the grass, punctuated by palms, drifts down to the water's edge. The house is divided into two separate structures. The bedroom wing houses children's rooms on the ground floor, together with an office and media room, hidden behind an arcade. Above this is the master suite with a private terrace overlooking the garden. On the other flanking side a vast palapa-roofed living and dining pavilion opens onto a front patio, which is used for alfresco meals and poolside lounging.

Ermenegildo's furniture choices are diverse and eclectic, mixing East and West with his own designs. These have a modernistic simplicity but blend well with the wide variety of Indonesian, Chinese, and African pieces grouped around the house in careful arrangements. Many of these come from the Galerie Nathalie Duchayne in Saint-Tropez. For the palapa living areas Ermenegildo built his customary cement banquettes upholstered with Mexican hand-loomed fabrics in yellow and orange. Color is limited to orange and yellow, and private rooms are a simple white. The one

■ Two views of the master bathroom. Ermenegildo designed the hand-made cement bathtub, which is flanked by antique ladders from the Philippines. The shower hangs from a peeled log that hides the plumbing.

exception that he allowed himself is a curved wall in the dining palapa that screens the kitchens and is finished in an unmistakable Mexican blue.

The house eventually became popular with the local international community, once they saw the advantages of its indoor-outdoor lifestyle and the harmoniously organic nature of its design. Ermenegildo is now embarking on another house in Casa de Campo for the same client. One day he may influence a whole new look for the region.

A row of tree trunks forms a natural barrier to the sea breezes in this outdoor seating area. Hand-loomed Mexican fabrics were used for the colorful cushions.

The main swimming pool overlooks the ocean. The elliptical shape of the pool is outlined by slight dips in the level of the surrounding paving. The entry to the pool is defined by a checkerboard of lawn and paving stones.

■ A poolside area near the house and protected by a pergola is where the owners like to entertain. PAGES 234–35: Aerial view of the Casa Pacifica.

index

acknowledgments

■ Carolina von Humboldt, Ahmad Sardar-Afkhami, Annie Kelly, Tim Street-Porter, and Manolo Mestre on an expedition to the Hacienda San José Carpizo.

WORKING ON THIS BOOK WAS A WONDERFUL journey through Mexico in the company of many good friends.

It all began with the enthusiasm of Jorge Almada and Anne-Marie Midy when we stayed with them in beautiful San Miguel de Allende. Their sophisticated Mexican sensibility was a great inspiration. We could not have done this book at all, however, without our friend Manolo Mestre, who has kept our love of Mexico alive for nearly twenty years.

Duccio Ermenegildo and Nicolle Meyer were our friends and inspiration in Careyes, and we instantly became friends with Anibal Gonzalez and Monica Hernandez when we stayed with them at the Hacienda Katanchel. They later sheltered us in their Villa Hanoi during Hurricane Emily, and that night, before the lights went out, the artist James Brown—our fellow refugee—gave us many helpful suggestions for the book. In Campeche, Manolo introduced us to Carlos Vidal, the head of the Centro INAH, who sent us out on an expedition to the wonderful Hacienda San José Carpizo.

In Los Angeles, our neighbors Sergio and Marie Nicolau were always on hand for advice; Mike Kelly provided our technical support; decorator Martyn Lawrence-Bullard gave us many helpful comments; and Gregorio Luke, the director of the Museum of Latin American Art in Long Beach, was an enthusiastic supporter. Charles Sanchez assisted Tim on a tour of Yucatán haciendas for English *Condé Nast Traveller* (and appears in several of the photographs). As always, Christin Markmann, Tim's office manager and assistant, was a wonderful support.

We were also helped by Alejandro Pelayo, Mexican Consul for Cultural Affairs, Los Angeles, who did all he could to make this book possible.

We are grateful to *Architectural Digest*, the most important magazine to cover Mexican architecture in such depth, for the use of some of the photos Tim has taken for them.

Thanks, finally, to all the owners of these beautiful houses who were kind enough to open them to us.